REBEL
THREADS

Best wishes

R.K. B——

Published in 2017 by The Horse Hospital
in association with Laurence King Publishing Ltd.

The Horse Hospital
Colonnade, Bloomsbury
London WC1N 1JD

popculture@thehorsehospital.com
www.thehorsehospital.com

A catalogue record for this book is
available from the British Library.

ISBN 978-1-78627-094-8

Book Design **William Burton**
Studio Photography **James Lyndsay**
Stylist **Roger K. Burton**
Assistant Stylist **Laura Nash**
Retouching **Laura Locke**
Editor **Helen Rochester**
Copy Editor **Richard Bancroft**
Proofreading **Cathi Unsworth**
Picture Research **Sandra Assersohn**
Printed in Estonia by **Tallinna Raamatutrükikoda**

Typeset in Trade Gothic and Benton Sans.

www.rebel-threads.com

REBEL THREADS

CLOTHING OF THE BAD, BEAUTIFUL & MISUNDERSTOOD

ROGER K. BURTON

Hugh Finnegan and his Teddy Boy mates meet before going on to Billy Mannings' Funfair. Back row L/R Albie Deacon, Eugeen Finnegan, Adrian Cutler, Barry Stewart and Buller Wilson, front row L/R Hugh Finnegan, Roger Sands, Alfie Gunner and big Robbie Patton. Sallyport, Old Portsmouth, 1955. Courtesy Hugh Finnegan.

FOREWORD

Once upon a time to be young meant you got to cast yourself in the movie of your own life. Rather than prioritising what job if you were lucky you might end up getting, you got to decide instead what kind of human being you wanted to be.

Whether you were you a Beat, a Mod, a Hippie or a Punk, you became part of a defiant youth tribe which defined itself around the potential of what you could be. You became energised by each other. Galvanised by the music, the attitude and above all the look of your own sub-culture. Instead of accepting the tired out, top-down ways of seeing and being, imposed on you by parents, government and school, you seized your place in your own magical and irreverent version of the world.

The portal to this adventure was of course the looking glass and the look you presented in front of it was the key to unlocking it. You were, above all, what you wore. Those rebel threads gained you access to the secret and arcane knowledge that lay beyond the mirror.

Roger Burton supplied the extensive wardrobe on *Absolute Beginners* from his own collection, dressing the extras with both loving exactitude and rule-breaking imagination. I remember vividly the mornings on that extraordinary Soho set of ours, when the London club kids arrived in all their mid 1980s finery, straight from wild all-nighters at the Wag and other Soho dives of the time, to undergo a miraculous transformation under Roger's supervision. He sent them back in time, re-emerging as immaculate, living, breathing Teds, Beats and Modernist denizens of late 1950s Soho, strutting their stuff on the Technicolor streets of our set as though they owned it.

The hair and clothes may have changed, clicking back through three decades, but that irreverent spirit of rebel youth remained the same. Suddenly I realised that despite all the disparate styles and attitudes so lovingly detailed in this book, our incandescent succession of youth cultures have all been part of something bigger than themselves. The art of being alive. The art of creating both yourself and the world you want to live in. One thing is for certain – we could sure do with a whole new run of those rebel threads right now.

Roger is the infinite collector and master curator of this living and wearable history. *Rebel Threads* provides eloquent and indispensable testimony to his enduring passion for and profound knowledge about what lies behind every stitch of these clothes that changed the world.

Julien Temple, Film Director

WHAT GOES AROUND...

Having spent most of my life collecting, wearing and styling vintage street fashion, I felt now was a good time to share my knowledge and passion for teenage sub-culture and get it into a book, especially as interest in vintage clothes is at an all-time high. It's been a journey of constant discovery and much personal involvement, so I've woven several of my own experiences into the chapters to add context to the clothes' history, and in this introduction I'll briefly explain how the collection came together.

The first major event I can remember was in 1953, when my parents bought a black and white TV set to watch the Queen's Coronation; I was four. Before long I, like most of my generation, was being fed a daily diet of Westerns, and swashbuckling TV series. I adored the fearless antics of *The Buccaneers*, *William Tell* and *Robin Hood*, and The Lone Ranger and Wyatt Earp were my heroes. I would dress up as a cowboy at any opportunity, and I remember desperately wanting Davy Crockett's raccoon tail hat; it took some persuasion for my mum to buy me a kid's version. I treasured that hat for years, and still have it.

The collecting bug first bit me around the age of eight. Being a farmer's son, I grew up with a weakness for farm machinery, and would find myself regularly writing away to manufacturers asking for enamel lapel badges like the salesmen wore at agricultural shows, which were way more impressive than the mass-produced tin variety liberally handed out to us kids.

Around this time my older sister was hooked on the latest rock 'n' roll music, which inevitably rubbed off on me, and by 1957 I had become infatuated with Elvis Presley. I loved everything about him, especially 'Hound Dog' and 'Jailhouse Rock'. I even joined his fan club.

Desperately wanting to be grown up, a couple of years later I was collecting, of all things, empty cigarette packets, usually exotic American brands I found in roadside lay-bys, discarded by local USAF airbase staff.

The big yearly pilgrimage was to a local fairground, with my mates. This intense exposure to loud rock 'n' roll music, and gangs of tough looking youths in leather jackets, looking cool under the neon lights, was incredibly cinematic and seductive to a youngster, but scary as hell.

By the early 1960s I was discovering the joys of R&B and soul music at the local youth club, and hanging out with likeminded Modernist kids. I had absolutely hated school and authority, and escaped as soon as I turned 15 in 1964. Throughout my teens I hoarded copies of *The Sunday Times Magazine*, and I'm sure they ended up supplementing my lack of education. I got a job on a farm and spent all my pitiful wages on clothes, and the weekends in dark dingy clubs, experiencing a heady rush from pep pills while dancing to soul music all night long. The Mod movement affected me so strongly that the philosophy of style I learnt then remains with me today.

By 1966 the Hippie 'thing' was taking a hold, so to counter it a few of us friends started wearing original 1930s and 1940s gangster style clothes like those worn by *The Untouchables*, a then popular American TV series set in Chicago during prohibition; bands The Purple Gang and local Leicester group Family, who we followed, were really into the look. I bought a chalk stripe demob suit and plundered my grandpa's wardrobe for period correct ties. To a purist Mod, the gangster look was a much more appealing alternative to dressing in Hippie robes, and was actually the beginning of an exciting revivalist journey.

I took a job in a factory driving a crane for a couple of years because it paid more money, but soon decided to go freelance, window cleaning, gardening and restoring antique furniture, in fact any odd job that came along. In the early 1970s there was a 1950s revival and again my friends and I got seriously into the clothes and music. In December 1972, *Esquire* magazine further endorsed the 1950s Americana look we all sought, with an article that featured everything from vintage zoot suits to stadium jackets and two-tone saddle shoes as the latest nostalgia fashion.

Street markets were usually the best source of original clothing, and I had a stall myself for some time, selling antiques and small collectables. I then took a lease on a shop in Leicester, calling it Pioneer Antiques, later Hollywood Fashions, and here I bought and sold old advertising signs, pub mirrors, stripped pine furniture, objects, tin toys, and vintage clothes. Quite soon clothes became my main source of income as London dealers found the shop, and I had to spend most of my time sourcing stock from flea markets and antique fairs. I found a likeminded partner in Birmingham and together we travelled up and down the country looking for vintage and dead stock period clothing, selling to a growing number of vintage shops in London and other cities around the world. By 1974 we were buying huge amounts of period clothes just to satisfy demand.

All eyes had been on Malcolm McLaren and Vivienne Westwood since they opened Let it Rock in 1971 at 430 Kings Road, selling 1950s vintage Teddy Boy clothes, and after a couple of other shop transformations they began cooking up an entirely new set of radical clothes designs, influenced by elements of clothing they had sold before. These designs had an attitude that fit perfectly with the new wave of angry Punk bands, and captured the imagination of the nation's youth. In 1975 Punk took the music and fashion worlds by storm, and gave the so-called blank generation a voice. Whether it was through wearing a black trash bin liner, and a safety pin through the lip; a DIY ripped-up school blazer; or an expensive tartan bondage suit from Seditionaries, it didn't matter. They were all singing the same anthem, 'Anarchy in the UK'.

Punk seriously damaged our vintage clothes business, but its spirit also inspired a positive reaction in people like myself, and instilled a new appreciation of eclectic styling that finally broke the period purist mould. As a reaction, we began buying military clothes from army surplus stores across Holland, Germany and France, then dying and modifying them. In 1978 we teamed up with two friends to open a clothes shop in Covent Garden called PX in which to sell the military clothes. I designed and built the shop in the style of an underground bunker, with industrial fittings I'd salvaged from the old MI5 building. But after a few months my old partner and I left, keen to start selling again, and set up a stall on Portobello Road, where fortuitously we were approached by an art director to supply as much authentic Mod clothing as we could find for The Who's new movie Quadrophenia. We had sold clothes to the production and on completion of the shoot, its producer suggested we buy them back and start a hire company specialising in vintage street fashion for the film,

TV and fashion industries. It made sense, as we still had a warehouse full of unsold vintage clothes, and had unknowingly kept the very best clothing examples for just such a purpose.

My design of the PX store had not gone unnoticed, and ironically in 1980 I was asked by McLaren and Westwood to redesign Seditionaries, the very shop that had been the catalyst of the Punk movement. Its replacement, Worlds End, became a cocktail of ideas drawn from the film The Cabinet of Dr Caligari and Alice in Wonderland, into an Olde Curiosity Shoppe for modern day pirates that would become a landmark in fashion history.

The following year I was again asked by McLaren and Westwood to design and build a second shop, called Nostalgia of Mud, in St Christopher's Place, London. Eclecticism ruled again, drawing from African mud huts, Regency architecture, sci-fi films and Second World War art. As McLaren later put it: 'These shops were beautiful stage sets, and never really designed to sell anything.' The shop was later heralded as the most innovative of the decade by Peter York, an influential style commentator of the time.

Meanwhile the new hire business, Contemporary Wardrobe, was just not happening until an article in The Sunday Times Magazine kick-started interest, and gradually the phone began to ring. Word spread about the collection through the Face, Blitz and i-D magazines, and before I knew it I was involved in the latest innovation from the music world, the pop video. 'Ghost Town' by the Specials was one of my first jobs, and I was soon being asked to dress new, upcoming and famous bands on a weekly basis. By the end of the 1980s I'd worked on several great movies, a series of cutting edge TV commercials, and styled well over 100 music videos.

In 1993 I moved the collection to an old Victorian Horse Hospital and launched the space with a retrospective exhibition of McLaren & Westwood's early Punk clothing. Since that time the space has gone on to host masses of diverse exhibitions and screened literally hundreds of underground films, and the clothes collection, which began with a mere handful of my grandpa's ties, has grown to some 20,000 items.

PREFACE

From teenage angst and rites of passage to dreams of changing the world, these fineries were once displayed with attitude and stance, by kids who'd rebel against anything you'd got... and generations who really believed they'd die before they got old...!

Rebel Threads is a celebration of those first generation bad, beautiful and misunderstood street punks who had nothing but each other, and the urge to belong to a gang or movement that offered the thrill of an alternative lifestyle, and the chance to set themselves apart from a boring mainstream society.

For me the story begins in America during the Great Depression of the 1930s, as groups of fanatical jazz fans all over the country started to emulate their heroes' style of dress at dances and on the street. Even though money was tight, kids were consumed by the scene and went mad for this new relaxed look which fit the music like a glove, and most importantly, was unlike anything their uptight forefathers had worn before.

From then on, street fashions linked to popular music would be a potent combination, and most of the early movements that followed the jazz scene were fuelled by the introduction of a new style of music, even though later sub-cultures would often appear as a reaction to the one before.

Additionally, while almost all of the sub-cultures featured in this book started out being anti-establishment and anti-authority, others were deliberately anti-fashion, or at least not fashion-led. But to say that none were influenced by fashion would be misleading, for within most sub-cultures or movements there are elements of the fashion of the day, and signs of conformity and uniformity that were coded and possibly only recognisable to others in that peer group; those subtle codes delineated their individual standing within their pack.

What seems clear from my research is that it was usually just a handful of switched-on hip kids within the various scenes, who would go out and cherry-pick clothing from stores or market stalls and style these items in such a way as to create their own distinct look, which in turn

encouraged others to follow their lead. However, with some of the more progressive movements, such as Mods, it is fair to say that as soon as too many kids copied or picked up on a particular style and made it fashionable, it would be quickly dropped by the originators.

My objective with this book is to show some of the best examples of those original street clothes styled in outfits as they were worn at the time. Wherever possible I have drawn from first-hand experience; the pre-1950s styles are based on extensive research and study of archive photos and historic documentary films. I have also attempted to trace the movements' origins, explain how they developed, related to each other and overlapped in style. Basically, I wanted to try and join the dots and illustrate how these originals paved the way for practically every other sub-cultural movement that followed.

The styling of the outfits is of course subjective and purely my own personal point of view, and I respect the fact that certain sub-cultures or movements in other countries, towns and even local areas will have worn their clothes in a different way, where these looks probably had different meanings. Lastly, while almost all of the items pictured in the groups are absolutely authentic and original, there are just a handful of very faithful reproductions included, as some of those items are so rare or ephemeral that the most resourceful researcher would be hard pressed to find an existing example, even in a museum.

As a stylist and costume designer myself, I am particularly interested in how street styles were depicted in movies of the time, and have included a selection of rare film stills, which in my view feature some of the most authentic costume styling. To add further context, I have also included selected images of kids and gangs wearing the clothes on the street. Original photographs like these are particularly hard to find, as very few teenagers seemed to own cameras or took photos of themselves until the 1970s, so I am particularly grateful to those who gave permission to use their personal photos.

INVISIBLE STRIPES

Striped shirts and tops have a long lineage of being associated with social outcasts such as pirates, prisoners and prostitutes, outlaws, gangsters, bikers and Beatniks. Almost all the sub-cultural and countercultural movements featured in this book have at some point along the way proudly worn stripes as a show of unity and rebelliousness.It was on the medieval battlefield where the stripe as a form of visual identification is likely to have first found prominence. Bold stripes, emblazoned on the heraldic tunics of knights, could be easily spotted by their opponents at great distances; likewise medieval court jesters and street entertainers wore striped costumes to stand out from the crowd.

Stripes were also used as warning signs at this time. Take the red and white spiral-striped barbers' poles. Aside from hair cuts and shaving, barbers also carried out blood-letting and tooth extraction; the pole therefore signified blood and bandages.

Stripes have a close association with the sea, and in the seventeenth century, merchant ships owned by the East India Company proudly flew a red-and-white striped ensign as they opened up important trading lanes around the globe.

Flags on naval and merchant ships not only identified the vessel, but a whole language of signs and signals developed from stripes, symbols and block colours to alert other ships of their intentions, or seaworthy condition.

In times of war during the seventeenth and eighteenth centuries, able-bodied men between the ages of 18 and 55 were regularly press-ganged to serve in the Royal Navy. Petty criminals too would often be given an option of volunteering for service in the navy instead of serving time in prison, and although life on board ship was harsh, it was probably better than a stretch behind bars.

As an easy way for officers to monitor their activities on board ship, seaman were issued with a bold striped top as part of their uniform. With so many men there against their will, they would sometimes become unruly, and this led to desertions and mutinies over poor pay and conditions. These offences were punishable by hanging.

Bold striped uniforms were also being utilised effectively on prison inmates, and this practical approach to surveillance is thought to have originated in America sometime in the 1700s. The combination of horizontal striped uniforms and vertical prison bars symbolically formed a fence or barrier, which in turn had a psychological effect on the prisoners, reiterating their threat to society.

In 1765 a group of angry Boston citizens, the Sons of Liberty, formed a rebellious underground organisation to protest against the Stamp Act and other unfair taxes being imposed by the British government on the colonies.

The standard they adopted was a red and white vertical striped flag, with nine bars to represent the 'loyal nine' original colonies who joined the rebels. Their often violent actions were very effective, and within two years four more states had joined the revolt, paving the way to America's independence. The flag they flew now had 13 red and white horizontal bars and became known as 'The Rebellious Stripes'. In 1777, this same formation would be forever integrated into the American 'Stars & Stripes' flag as recognition of the Sons of Liberty.

For centuries what a person wore, either at work or play, was an easily recognisable symbol of their standing in an ordered society. But within four short years these outdated views were to be broken down and all but thrown out of the window, firstly by the protesting Hippie movement of the late 1960s, and then ten years later in 1976 by the new wave anarchists and the Punk movement. These would eventually give way to today's bland, homogenised, consumer society, where all but a few remaining movements' fashion and dress codes have lost their former relevance and respect.

Scorpio Rising, dir Kenneth Anger, 1964.

1

SO WHAT!

SWING KIDS, HEP CATS & BOBBY SOXERS

MID 1930s – MID 1950s

"We cannot always build a future for our youth,
but we can always build our youth for the future."

Franklin D. Roosevelt, 1940.

By the mid 1930s, a nationwide mania for the latest jazz music and Hollywood movies was sweeping across America and simultaneously helping the country to drive its way out of the doldrums of Depression. These phenomena fuelled the American Dream and captured the hearts and minds of young people, with their fantasy visions of modern times, carefree lifestyles and taste for freedom. Forward-thinking planners, architects and designers were all busy looking to the future with a new wave of collective optimism.

Exciting fashions inspired by the stars of movies and swing music aimed at a younger market emerged and, with the launch of *The March of Time* newsreel in 1935 and *Life* magazine in 1936, a new era of mass communication had begun, bringing pictorial news and views of the world to every American doorstep.

American tailors in the early 1930s had learnt to adapt to less affluent times by producing suits that were generally shorter and leaner in cut. Then, in 1935, Savile Row tailor Frederick Scholte created the 'London cut' (or 'drape cut' as it was known), which featured a much fuller silhouette, with broad shoulders, wide lapels, a long, full, double-breasted jacket and wide-leg trousers. The style had instant appeal for American men, in fact, so much so that it was renamed the 'American cut' or 'V-line'.

Are you Hep to Jive?

Around the same time that jazz icon Cab Calloway was lighting-up radio airwaves, flashy images appeared of him in the press displaying a new style of oversized outfit nicknamed the zoot suit, which would turn the heads of young guys searching for a look to call their own. The zoot suit was, in fact, a highly exaggerated version of the American cut.

Arguably created in Harlem, jackets were double- or single-breasted and knee length, similar in proportion to a Victorian frock coat, but a much looser cut: huge shoulders, extreme draped back, extra-wide peaked lapels, and high-waist peg top trousers, which ballooned at the knee, dramatically tapering down to the ankle, finishing with a gathered cuff. The entire look was promoted as a 'novelty style', and quickly taken up by young black and Hispanic men, who tended to wear it in a relaxed, casual way almost like sportswear, which was ideal for dancing in.

It must have been quite exceptional for young people to have enough money to afford extravagant clothes at this time, but it was clearly worth the high price to these kids, as zoot suits became the first real street style to catch on in America. A new casual attitude to dress was developing, liberating teenagers from traditional adult constraints, like the formality of a suit worn with a stiff shirt collar and tie. Adopting these outlandish outfits helped establish a new order and, most importantly, they served as a uniform of rebellion.

Previous page: The Dead End Kids, John Garfield and Gloria Dickson, *They Made me a Criminal*, dir Busby Berkeley, 1939.

Left: Fig 1. Navy wool worsted blazer, 1940s, England. Cream cotton blouse, 1940s, England. Maroon linen trousers, 1940s, England. Red leather wedge sandals, 1940s, England.

Fig 2. Navy and white striped cotton shirt, 1940s, England. Charcoal grey pleated wool skirt, 1940s, England. Black cotton socks. Black leather open toe sandals, 1940s, England.

Fig 3. Chocolate brown wool floral Tyrolean style cardigan, 1940s, Austria. Light grey wool swing skirt with yellow window pane check, 1940s, England. Black cotton socks. Red leather sandals, 1940s, Mansfield, England.

Fig 4. White and green striped rayon blouse, 1940s, England. Black wool swing skirt, 1940s, USA. Green cotton socks. White nu-buck sandals, 1940s, England.

Fig 5. Rust wool floral Tyrolean style sweater, 1940s, England. Grey and black fleck rayon swing skirt, 1940s, USA. Grey cotton socks. Cream leather sandals, 1940s, England.

Below: Deputy Sheriff Bartley Brown of East Los Angeles Police inspects the haircut of prisoner Alex 'Largo' Rodriguez, who is wearing an $85 zoot suit, June 7th 1943.

Right: Fig 1. Black and pale grey chalk stripe wool zoot jacket, late 1940s, Kenneway, Kensington, London. The unusual stripe configuration on this jacket was no doubt influenced by a frock coat worn by Clark Gable in *Gone With The Wind*, 1939. Grey-green gabardine shirt 1940s, Penneys Towncraft, USA. Green twill trousers, early 1950s, England. Black leather hoop stitched novelty shoes 1940s, USA. Metal key chain.

Fig 2. Cinnamon gabardine jacket, 1940s, Penneys Sports, USA. Rust and bisque striped T-shirt, 1940s, USA. Black gabardine trousers, early 1950s. Black leather Oxford toecap shoes, 1940s, England.

Fig 3. Two-tone grey cotton cardigan, 1940s, England. Black gabardine shirt, early 1950s, USA. Black gabardine trousers, early 1950s, England. Black leather crepe-soled shoes, early 1950s, 'Silver Leaf', American Italian Styled by Piago, late 1940s, England.

Fig 4. Grey worsted Zoot suit, c1947, N Salt, London. Black and cream striped T-shirt, cotton, mid 1980s, Beat-Beat London. Black leather Oxford toecap shoes, 1940s, England.

Fig 5. Beige and brown twill cardigan, 1940s, England. Cream rayon shirt, 1940s, USA. Chestnut wool trousers, 1940s, USA. Brown leather crepe-soled shoes 'Silver Leaf' American Italian Styled by Piago, late 1940s, England. Metal key chain.

Zoot suit wearers were often members of gangs, originally of young black men, but as the look spread across America, Mexicans known as Chicanos took to the style. In Los Angeles, gangs of Mexican American Pachucos were particularly into the look. Zoot suit derivatives were also worn by young women, and two gangs in particular – the 'Black Widows' and the 'Slick Chicks' – were noted by the press for wearing long black zoot-suit jackets with short black skirts, black fishnet stockings and heavy make-up.

The New York World's Fair opened in 1939 and provided people a glimpse into the future with the commercial debut of television. The movie *Gone with the Wind*, 1939, gave sell-out cinema audiences a Technicolor view of a romantic past, starring Vivien Leigh and Clark Gable, who sports a period frock coat with similar lines to the fashionable zoot suit.

The style seemed to fit perfectly with the mad dance crazes of the 1930s, such as the lindy hop, jitterbug, swing and jive variations, which at times would reach fever pitch. Harlem music halls such as the Cotton Club, the Savoy and the Apollo, became catwalks for the zoot suit, and it was here in the early 1940s that a young Malcolm X picked up on the look and had his own zoot suit tailor-made. He describes: 'a zoot suit with a reet pleat, with a drape shape'.

As the craze for swing music grew in the early 1940s, so the zoot suit gained in popularity, also now with white youths. Their suits became even more extreme, featuring wide stripes and large-checked fabrics, and long key chains that reached the ankle. Shirts, too, had extra-long, spear-point collars, and these would be styled with vividly printed or hand-painted ties and splayed hankies. Massive floppy bow-ties became a fad for a while, and the entire look was topped off with a pork pie hat – with its wide brim and low flat crown, this classic became the trademark of jazz musician and zoot suit wearer Lester Young. On stage, Cab Calloway would use light-coloured fabric in his wildly exaggerated outfits to over-emphasise his already larger than life image. Calloway was said to own over 40 custom-made outrageous outfits, and changed as many as 12 times during a performance, to the delight of his multitude of fans. In 1939, Calloway even wrote a *Hepster's Dictionary* about the language of jive. In 1943, a comedy movie called *Jitterbugs* was released starring Laurel and Hardy, who both wear exaggerated zoot suits, implying that the look should not be taken too seriously by normal folk.

Riots

America entered the Second World War in December 1941, and the American government imposed rationing measures from March 1942. Among other things, the manufacture of men's suits that required an excessive use of cloth was banned, and explicitly, no cuffs or pleats at the waist were allowed on any wool trousers. But demand for zoot suits from youngsters remained high, and many tailors continued to make them illegally.

Discrimination was rife during the interwar period, and among teenagers finding their feet for the first time there was a growing feeling of resentment, particularly by young black and Hispanic kids, who were victims of racial prejudice and lack of freedom.

By 1943, feelings were running so high that they resulted in a series of violent disturbances that became known as the Zoot Suit Riots. Gangs of youths would deliberately flaunt the look, which to them was a symbol of freedom, racial identity and a protest against what they saw as a senseless war. This attitude incensed patriotic Americans, and led to packs of serviceman and vigilante citizens taking to the streets to challenge anyone wearing the look. That summer, a full-scale riot took place in Los Angeles. Reports were widespread of individuals being stripped of their expensive suits, which were then cut to shreds or burnt, with the wearer either beaten up or publicly humiliated by being left naked in the street. Tension grew, and the gangs retaliated with vicious fighting that lasted for several weeks and involved hundreds of young men from both sides. The Los Angeles police eventually called in 1,000 extra officers to restore order. After numerous arrests, police records revealed that many of the gangs' members were directly involved in drug dealing and theft. Claims were also made that it was the cash obtained from these illicit activities that enabled the zoot suit revellers to afford their expensive clothes.

Right: Teenagers during the Zoot Suit Riots, Los Angeles, 1943.

Zah Zuh Zah

Swing music was also incredibly popular in Europe, and by the early 1940s groups of notorious young Parisian men collectively known as the Zazous began wearing a similar look to the zoot suit with their long, drape-style jackets. The Zazous' style actually bore closer resemblance to English Teddy Boys, predating them by a good ten years, with their stove-pipe trousers worn short with turn-ups, a good four inches above thick-soled suede shoes, to show off white or brightly coloured socks. Zazous also preferred narrower ties, with subtle patterns, often worn with striped, high-collar, pin-through shirts. Reputedly, they were never seen without sunglasses, had long hair, and would carry furled umbrellas. Like the Beatniks and Existentialists, they too hung around smoky bars in the Latin Quarter, and were said to drink their own style of cocktail, a mixture of beer and grenadine.

The Zazous' style continued to be popular until the middle of the Second World War, when it gradually faded out. This was largely due to mounting pressure from the authorities to stamp out its flagrant decadence. The French public saw the Zazous as unpatriotic, and as in America, victimisation and beatings took place. As a further humiliation, several scalpings occurred. Hair had become a valuable commodity, and a vital component in the manufacture of slippers.

Before the War, Germany too had its own interpretation of the look based on the American model: its followers were known as 'Swing Kids'. England also played host to the zoot suit from the mid-1940s, where it was mainly seen around jazz circles after being introduced to the country by American servicemen. It was a hot item on the black market and master tailors were said to be alarmed when the style was spotted just a mile from Savile Row. But the English version never seriously caught on, and remained almost exclusively underground. The Zazous, however, would appear again very briefly after the War, as did the zoot suit as a minor fashion in America, but by then much of the old spirit had gone out of the movements, and both soon lost favour to new styles.

Above: 1. Tan leather and cream nu-buck saddle shoes, 1950s, Weber Sports, USA. White cotton socks and black leather dog collar. During the 1950s one of many short-lived US fads saw dog collars being worn by teenage girls on the left ankle, to indicate that the girl had a boyfriend, and on the right ankle to show she was single.

2. Brown felt trilby hat, 1940s, USA.

Left: Fig 1. Brown wool stadium jacket with cream knitted shawl collar, 1950s, USA. Green and brown wool plaid shirt, 1960s, VIP, USA. Khaki chinos, 1950s, USA. Tan leather cowboy boots by Brooks Boots, 1960s, USA.

Fig 2. Red and black shadow check zip-up wool jacket, 1950s, USA. White and red waffle weave top, 1950s, USA. Blue denim side zip jeans, 1950s, USA. White cotton socks. Black leather crepe-soled loafers with white stitching, 1950s, Kiltie by Norvic, England.

Angels With Dirty Faces

Movie theatres, with their production-line films and weekly newsreels, were very much the internet of the time, and impressionable teenagers around the globe were quick to pick up on catchy American slang and copy movie stars' styles of clothing, as they became enthralled by this seductive medium. They relished the cinema's eternal promise of escapism through romantic tales of heroic feats and rebelliousness, and as films were a relatively cheap form of entertainment in the depressed 1930s, it was not uncommon for kids to go to the cinema two or three times a week. Darkened cinema aisles were also discreet places where couples could go on dates hidden away from parents' prying eyes, and as the studios subsequently cottoned on to the fact that teenagers had their own money to spend, so they became a new target audience.

In 1935, movie producer Sam Goldwyn and director William Wyler went to see a New York theatre production of *Dead End* about a gang of low-class juvenile delinquent kids growing up on the streets of New York, and decided to make the story into a film. *Dead End* the movie opened in 1937 and began a long series of gritty social realism films starring the 'Dead End Kids', which were extremely successful and featured famous character actors such as tough guys John Garfield and Humphrey Bogart. One of the best known of the series is *Angels with Dirty Faces*, 1938, starring James Cagney.

Around the same time, but at the other end of the social spectrum, a family movie called *Love Finds Andy Hardy*, 1938, starring Mickey Rooney and Judy Garland, went on general release. The film was the fourth in the popular 'Andy Hardy' series and the third with the young Rooney, who had that 'boy-next-door' appeal. This new pairing with Garland firmly established them as Hollywood's first teenage couple.

Rooney and Garland both exuded star quality and projected good wholesome American values. Through their films, they showed that with pure determination and enthusiasm anything was possible, and this morale-raising attitude was exactly what was needed to lift teenagers out of the doldrums.

A string of hit films starring the duo was released and their following grew to enormous proportions, with kids right across the country emulating the clean-cut image of their heroes. In New York, thousands of frenzied fans stopped the traffic outside the premiere of the 1939 film *The Wizard of Oz* just to catch a glimpse of their idols, even though Rooney did not appear in the film.

White American boys had been slower to respond to the extremes of the zoot suit style, preferring the more wholesome sports-casual collegian styles that were then being promoted for boys and girls. Check shirts, striped T-shirts, short gabardine jackets, baseball jackets, varsity cardigans, denim jeans, chino pants, wide-leg slacks, baseball boots and loafers were popular with both sexes, with the addition of figure-hugging blouses, sweaters, straight and pleated A-line skirts, and two-tone saddle shoes worn with white ankle socks by the girls. The nicknames 'Bobby Soxers' for girls and 'Hep Cats' for guys had become all the rage by 1937.

T-shirts seem to have been around forever but, aside from being a standard component of the military uniform, it wasn't really until the mid 1940s that they began to be worn as outer garments in America. In 1949, *City Across The River* became one of the first films to tell the story of a tough teenage street gang – the Amboy Dukes from Brooklyn, who all wore T-shirts as part of their look. The film was also good-looking gang member Tony Curtis's big break, and his slicked-back hairstyle would be used as a model look for teenage boys all over the world well into the 1960s. But it took Marlon Brando in *A Streetcar Named Desire*, 1951, to really make T-shirts a desirable item of clothing and thus a staple in every teenager's wardrobe.

Clothing endorsed by famous movie stars and singers such as Frank Sinatra meant guaranteed sales to teenage fans, and the influence of fashion seen in movies at this time was so great that many designers and manufacturers moved to California to produce a whole range of Hollywood-inspired clothes. Even though these companies had no real connection with the industry, a Los Angeles address would be sure to increase demand. Within a few years Hollywood had reached its peak, and California had become America's main manufacturing base for leisure and sports fashion.

Left: Fig 1. Indigo and white chalk stripe gabardine suit, 1951, JC Field & Sons, Chicago. White cotton shirt with collar pin, 1950s, USA. Navy, red and pink abstract splash print silk tie, 1950s, Stetson, USA. This suit was worn by Terry Hall of The Specials, in the 1981 video 'Ghost Town', also by Ray Davies of The Kinks, in the 1983 video 'Come Dancing'.

Fig 2. Black crepe swing dress with sequins detail on crimson panels, 1940s, Syd Juniors, USA. Black patent platform peep-toe shoes, 1940s, 'Marlone Continental Styling', England.

Above: Swing dancing couple, Savoy Ballroom, Harlem, 1947.

Right: Fig 1. Cream and grey striped rayon dress, early 1950s, USA. Black suede stiletto heel court shoes, early 1950s, by Fredericks of Hollywood.

Fig 2. Pistachio fleck gabardine Bold Look style suit, early 1950s, Rocket 55 by Winchester, USA. Cream rayon Mr B style shirt, early 1950s, USA. Gold weave rayon tie, early 1950s, Duratye, England. Gilt domino tie clip, early 1950s, England. Black leather crepe-soled shoes, late 1940s, 'Silver Leaf' American Italian Styled by Piago, England.

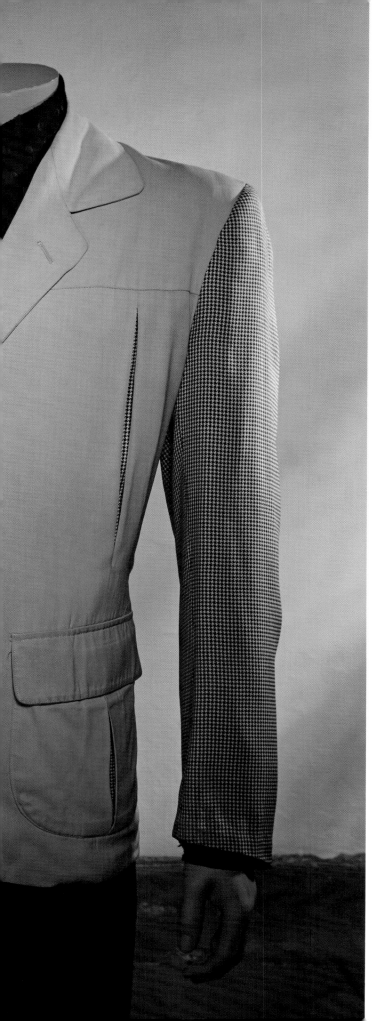

Rebel Without a Cause

In 1950, *Your Hit Parade* appeared for the first time on American TV. A radio favourite with teenagers since 1935, the show brought with it the latest rock 'n' roll stars, and heartthrobs like Frankie Laine, Johnnie 'Cry' Ray and Billy Eckstine, who stole the hearts of teenagers across America.

A new 'Bold Look' for men had been featured in *Esquire* magazine for a couple of years, and this reworking of the zoot suit and V-line with its looser, longer-length, draped jacket, extra-wide lapels and broad shoulders accentuated the V shape. Again it became a big hit with jazz musicians and the new wave of doo-wop bands and crooners who took the look to extremes. The style came in a new exotic range of flecks, slubs and gabardine fabrics that were available in a myriad of bright colours and pastel shades. Famous jazz trumpeter Billy Eckstine even designed a unique flex-roll, cutaway-collar shirt and called it 'Mr B' to go with the 'Bold Look'. He developed the shirt for himself to accommodate the swelling of his neck when he played the trumpet. It featured a loose, deep-roll collar, which fastened much lower down the neck than normal shirts, giving greater freedom and a unique look that also emphasised the tie. Within a couple of years, English Teddy Boys and Girls would adopt this style of shirt too.

This was the golden age of ties, which became a vivid canvas of expression; print designs changed weekly, and all types of famous artists and designers were commissioned to produce the most bizarre abstract and figurative scenes. Anything was possible, and the more ties screamed for attention, the more they sold. Wide, short, silk or rayon ties were most popular, but bow-ties, cravats, pocket hankies and scarves of all shapes also got the vivid print treatment and became big sellers (unlike the narrow, square-ended ties in subdued colours that were mostly sought after by the jazz fraternity).

Left: Fig 1. Brown and cream salt and pepper tweed sports jacket with cinnamon suedette breast panels, 1950s, USA. Cream cotton shirt, 1950s, USA. Yellow, pink and brown hand painted rayon tie with floating kinetic inspired mesh discs, 1940s, Pilgrim Cravats, USA.

Fig 2. Yellow ochre gabardine Hollywood style jacket with black and yellow ochre houndstooth sleeves and inserts, early 1950s, Irvine Foster, Miami Beach. Black rayon shirt, 1950s, USA. Yellow silk tie with red signet print, 1950s, Moorlane Foulard, England.

Early 1950s America was on the up economically, kids had money in their pockets, and in every sense, bigger was promoted as better. Body-conscious young men began emulating the beefcake physiques of Charles Atlas and Mickey Hargitay. Pin-up Sweater Girls such as Lana Turner, Marilyn Monroe and Betty Page all posed in provocative underwear, and this sent lingerie specialist Frederick's of Hollywood into production overdrive with a fantastic range of wired conical bras and sculptural corsetry to enhance the look.

Calf-length circular, dirndl-style skirts, also referred to as the 'conversation circle' or 'poodle skirts', were adopted by every young jiver and campus dweller. They came in a wide variety of fabrics and bright colours, with felt being very popular. The skirts, which were worn cinched in tight with a thick belt to form a wasp-like waist, were often decorated with embroidered appliqué motifs, such as clowns, musical notes, poodles and dancing figures highlighted with fur and rhinestones. In just a few years, circular skirts would become an essential part of rock 'n' roll attire around the world.

There were many fads and micro-fashions that caught on. One fad had girls wearing a dog collar over their ankle socks, on the right leg for a single girl, and on the left leg for those with boyfriends.

Rock 'n' roll was publically denounced by God-fearing folk as the Devil's music, and the press regularly ran stories of crazy, mixed-up kids who were under its spell, out of control and posing a genuine threat to an ordered society.

As a result, film studios began producing low-budget B-movies targeting the youth market. These films featured a new crop of attractive teenage heartthrobs groomed by the studios and dressed in clothes just like the styles of neighbourhood kids. Screenplays typically depicted teenage angst and rebellion, and the trials of growing up. Invariably the influence of these films spilled onto the streets, attracting gangs of young free-thinking and sometimes unruly teenage fans who hung out on street corners, acting out scenarios they had just seen at the movies, all vying for attention.

Right: Fig 1. Cherry red corduroy suit, early 1950s, H&D Fashions, USA.

Fig 2. Navy blue slub linen jacket, 1950s, Xavier Cugat Day & Night Coat, USA. Grey cotton button-down collar shirt, 1950s, USA. Navy silk hand-painted tie with red leaves and white Chihuahua, 1950s, X Cugat USA.

Above: The Amboy Dukes gang, Tony Curtis's screen debut (third from the left), *City Across The River*, dir Maxwell Shane, 1949.

Right: Fig 1. Cream wool swagger back coat, mid 1950s, USA. Pale lilac wool cardigan with white broderie anglaise trim, mid 1950s, De Pinna, 5th Avenue New York. Deep lilac pleated skirt, mid 1950s, USA. Bone leather stiletto shoes, mid 1950s, Lavor Artigiana, Italy.

Fig 2. Red cotton Harrington jacket, mid 1950s, USA. White cotton T-shirt, USA. Blue denim Levi's 501 jeans, USA. Black leather biker boots, mid 1950s, USA.

Fig 3. Black wool jacket with dice weave, mid 1950s, Curlee Sportswear, USA. White oxford cotton button-down collar shirt, mid 1950s, Brooks Brothers, USA. Brown wool trousers, mid 1950s, England. Black leather loafers, USA.

This generally innocent action was eventually seen as a threat to grown-ups and the establishment alike. Filmmakers were soon being pressured by the authorities to present storylines with moralistic endings that highlighted the perils of juvenile delinquency and covered everything from illicit drug use to reckless driving, with the inevitable consequences of fast living.

Cult films, such as *A Streetcar Named Desire*, 1951, and *The Wild One*, 1953, starring the sultry Marlon Brando; *Blackboard Jungle*, 1955, featuring Sidney Poitier; *Rebel Without a Cause*, 1955, played by James Dean; and *The Violent Years*, 1956, with Jean Moorhead, were almost certainly aimed at deterring a repeat of the riots and uprisings that happened during the early 1940s.

Left: Fig 1. Navy and white check fleck jacket, mid 1950s, USA. White rayon shirt, mid 1950s, USA. Black wool trousers, mid 1950s, England. Brown leather shoes with beige basket weave inserts, mid 1950s, USA.

Fig 2. Pale pink satin dress with black floral flock print, Colleen Originals, mid 1950s, USA. Brown leather loafers, mid 1950s, Ellaine, England.

Fig 3. Black hailstone fleck jacket, mid 1950s, USA. Lettuce gabardine shirt, The Duke, mid 1950s, USA. Heather green twill trousers, mid 1950s, England. Black leather loafers, USA.

Fig 4. Purple gabardine jacket with blue front panels and red and white diamonds, Ensenada, mid 1950s, USA. Red cotton sports shirt with chrome toggle fastening, mid 1950s, Fischers of London. Duck egg blue twill peg top trousers, mid 1950s, USA. Black and white suede loafers, mid 1950s, USA.

Fig 5. Cream wool top with heavy gold embroidered flowers, mid 1950s, USA. Copper corset belt with gold lace rope tie, 1958, England. British starlet Diana Dors was photographed wearing an identical corset belt in 1958. Cream cotton cropped trousers, mid 1950s, England. Cream and gold lace peep toe stilettoes, Desiree by Lotus, mid 1950s, England. Cream ruched nylon gloves, mid 1950s, England. Heavy gilt bracelets, mid 1950s, USA.

But there was no stopping this teenage revolution and demand for rock 'n' roll films took centre stage throughout the decade, with movies like *Rock Around the Clock*, 1956, with Bill Haley; *The Girl Can't Help It*, 1956, with a star-studded cast that included Little Richard, Eddie Cochran and Jayne Mansfield; Elvis Presley in *Jailhouse Rock*, 1957; and *High School Confidential*, 1958, with Russ Tamblyn and Mamie Van Doren, culminating in the ultimate teenage gang film, *West Side Story*, 1961, starring Natalie Wood and Richard Beymer.

By the mid 1950s, California had become a role model and vast playground for teenagers obsessed with endless up-to-date fashions, fads and the latest dance crazes. The state epitomised the new teenage culture, with its wild surfing beaches, Disneyland, bowling alleys, drive-ins, diners, drag strips, drugstores and Wurlitzer-driven 'Juke Joints', which all served as essential places for kids to meet and hang out, see the latest fashions, hear the latest sounds, and most importantly, spread the word.

Some films would continue to influence fashion, and fashions influence films, well until the 1960s, when TV took over the lead as a new, more immediate source of inspiration, turning films into more of a retrospective medium.

Right: Fig 1. Coffee linen jacket with beige and black striped front, mid 1950s, USA. Cream raw silk shirt with gold lurex thread, mid 1950s, Schenley of California.

Fig 2. Green and red tartan wool top and matching circle skirt, mid 1950s, Holyrood, Scotland. White cotton Bobby sox. Tan leather and cream nu-buck saddle shoes, 1940s, Weber Sports, USA.

Fig 3. Duck egg blue wool cardigan, mid 1950s, USA. Red, navy, blue and white fleck wool hobble skirt, mid 1950s, USA. White Bobby sox. Black leather and white nu-buck suede saddle shoes, mid 1950s, Town Flair, USA.

Fig 4. Brown, rust and cream argyle wool top, mid 1950s, England. Red brown and yellow fleck hobble skirt, mid 1950s, Laddies, USA. White cotton Bobby sox. Tan leather and white nu-buck suede saddle shoes, mid 1950s, J M Weston, France.

Fig 5. Black wool stadium jacket with red trim, mid 1950s, USA. Cream pink and grey wide pleated wool skirt, mid 1950s, USA. White Bobby sox. Black leather and white nu-buck suede saddle shoes, mid 1950s, Biltrite, USA.

Above: *The Violent Years*,
dir William M Morgan, 1956.

Right: Coffee linen jacket with beige and
black striped front, mid 1950s, USA.
Cream raw silk shirt with gold lurex
thread, mid 1950s, Schenley of California.

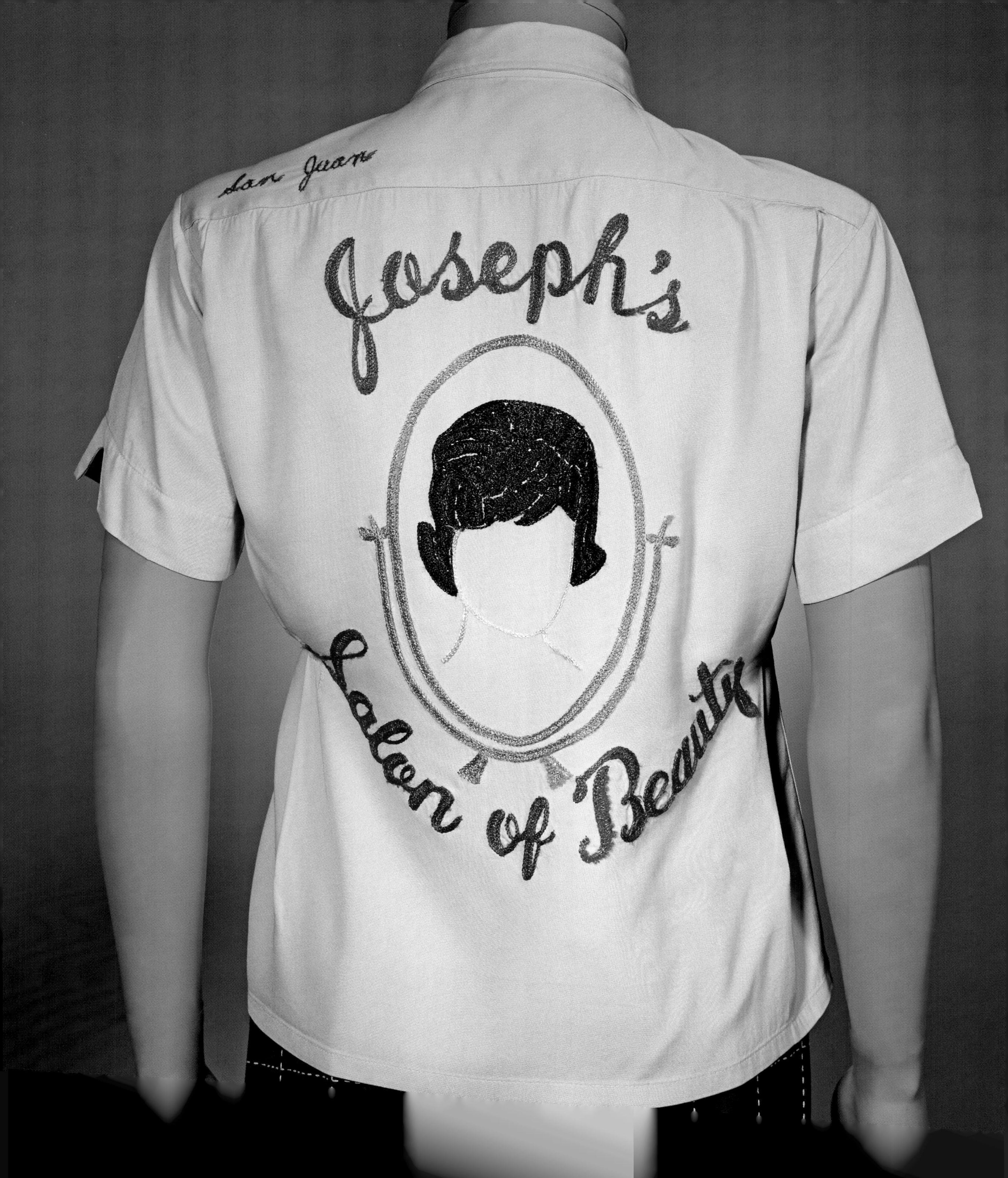
San Juan
Joseph's
Salon of Beauty

Left: Pink cotton bowling shirt with beauty salon embroidery, mid 1950s, USA. Black gabardine skirt with white saddle stitching, mid 1950s, USA.

Above: At Eagle Mountain Dragstrip, Texas, A Y Owen, 1957.

Left: Fig 1. Blue rayon track jacket with red and white off set stripe, 1960s, Swingster, USA. White cotton jeans, 1960s, Levi's 501, USA.

Fig 2. Peach cotton blouse, late 1950s, England. Peach vinyl belt. Peach, white, pink and black ten-pin bowling print skirt, late 1950s, England. White Bobby sox. Brown leather loafers, USA.

Fig 3. Yellow cotton track jacket with red and blue off set stripes, 1960s, Swingster, USA. Blue denim jeans, Levi's 501.

2

MR BIG SHOT

SPIVS & WIDE BOYS

EARLY 1940s – MID 1950s

"Londoners and other city dwellers will recognize him, so will many city magistrates – the slick, flashy, nimble-witted tough, talking sharp slang from the corner of his mouth. He is a sinister by-product of big-city civilisation – counterpart to the zoot-suited youths of America."

Bill Naughton, "Meet the Spiv", *News Chronicle*, 1945.

The criminal underworld is renowned for turning out larger-than-life characters, and many of these men will be particularly remembered for the way they dressed. One such rare bird was the British Spiv. Also referred to as 'Wide Boys' and 'Drones', these deft, draft-dodging entrepreneurs were most active during and just after the Second World War, where they could be seen working the black market in towns and cities up and down the country.

Looking for all the world like notorious 1920s and 1930s gangsters, such as Al Capone or Bugsy Siegel, in their often loud and flashy suits, Spivs are most likely to have originated back in the 1890s among racetrack gangs. The word 'Spiv' appears to be linked to 'spiff' or 'spiffy' – meaning neat or spruce – and the mid-nineteenth-century slang term 'spiff' – the commission given to a salesman by shopkeepers who wished to dispose of old stock. The *Cambridge Dictionary* definition: 'Spiv, a man, especially one who is well dressed in a way that attracts attention, who makes money dishonestly.' There is also a common theory that the name 'Spiv' is actually based on the acronym VIPs spelled backwards, and this would certainly seem to fit with their exclusive image.

Although Spivs as a sub-culture were never considered to be a youth movement, like many other illustrious villains, they shared the desire to stand out from the crowd and display their wealth and affluence through similar flamboyant dress codes. There is also no doubt that their influence on men's street fashions throughout the 1940s and early 1950s was considerable.

During the 1940s, the War effort would become a priority in most people's daily lives. Adults were issued with ration books in 1939 and, for the first time, rationing on goods such as petrol was imposed by the British government.

Also, other than uniforms, very few garments were manufactured at this time, and styles were limited in order to save cloth and materials. All items of clothing that were produced bore the CC41 utility stamp and were required to meet a government standard. Restrictions on the number of pockets on a garment and the length of men's shirts were imposed, while turn-ups on trousers were not permitted at all. In effect, the CC41 utility label led people to believe they were actually wearing a civilian uniform.

For most normal working people, being able to buy new clothes, let alone fashionable outfits, was an absolute luxury. Everyone was encouraged to 'make do and mend' the clothes they had bought before the War. By exploiting this unique situation, Spivs, whose main dealings involved supplying the unattainable, offered a ray of hope to many members of a fashion-hungry public who craved more than basic necessities to help make life during wartime a bit more bearable.

'Some call it bootlegging. Some call it racketeering. I call it a business. I am like any other man. All I do is supply a demand'. (Al Capone).

Supply & Demand

Alongside dead or fire-damaged stock obtained from wholesalers and retailers who had gone out of business because of the War, there were plenty of goods available that may have been acquired by more dubious means, such as 'falling off the back of a lorry'. West End robberies and smash-and-grab raids of jewellery and furs increased in London during the Blitz, as thieves were able to work with relative ease under cover of darkness in the blackout, particularly if the then short-staffed police force was having to deal with fires caused by German bombing raids in the far-off East End.

Having access to rare American merchandise was also a key factor in the Spivs' success. These so called 'little luxury' items, such as cigarettes, chewing gum, nylon stockings, and nail polish were regularly brought into Britain by newly stationed American servicemen, and rapidly became a popular racket on the black market.

As the War progressed and more and more servicemen were drafted over, so the Spivs, who bought directly from the visitors, thrived. And as rationing on many items was still imposed until 1954, so this underground trading continued unabated until well after the War was over.

Another regular source of coveted merchandise arrived via the luxury transatlantic Cunard liners that operated between Southampton and New York both before and after the War. For the well-heeled few that could afford to travel on them, these giant floating hotels had their own on-board entertainment, supplied by well-known British jazz bands of the time. The bands were mostly made up from session musicians, who made regular trips across the Atlantic, and these became known as Geraldo's Navy, after the famous BBC radio bandleader Geraldo, who acted as their agent and main supplier. The bands were extremely popular and played their part in bringing the latest swing and bebop sounds, dances and fashions from America to England.

Previous page: Richard Attenborough and Carol Marsh, *Brighton Rock*, dir John Boulting, 1947.

Right: Fig 1. Tan and brown tweed suit with shadow Prince of Wales check, 1940s, England. Blue cotton spear point collar shirt, 1940s, Banner CC41, England. Grey, blue and red fancy bowtie, 1940s, England.

Fig 2. Navy striped suit, 1946, C F Hoggett & Son, Leicester. Navy wool tank top with yellow stripes, 1940s, CC41. White striped spear point collar shirt 1940s, England. Ginger and tan plaid tie, 1940s, Klipper Tie, USA. Pearl tie pin.

Fig 3. Deep red swagger back wool coat with black stripes, 1940s, England. Pale blue white fine houndstooth cotton dress, 1940s, England. White plastic belt. Round gold locket, 1940s, England, kindly loaned by Laura Nash.

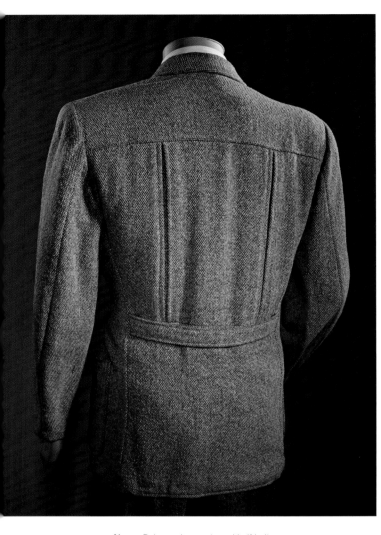

Above: Beige and green tweed half belt jacket with back pleat detail, 1950s, England.

Right: Fig 1. Brown and cream windowpane check wool overcoat, 1940s, England. White spear point collar shirt, 1940s, England. Brown and cream planetary print tie, 1940s, Linosair, England. Brown wool trousers, 1940s, England. Brown leather Oxford toe-cap shoes, 1940s, England.

Fig 2. Blue and navy window pane check wool overcoat, 1940s, England. Grey stripe spear point collar shirt, 1940s, England. Blue electric flash print tie, 1940s, Duratye, England. Navy wool trousers, 1940s, England. Black leather Oxford toe-cap shoes, 1940s, England.

While waiting for their next assignment on board a liner, band members would often hang out in London's Soho district at popular music venues. The area had always had a seedy low-life reputation and was a notorious location for clip joints, nudie revue bars and illegal drugs. It attracted many servicemen on leave with fresh pay packets, and so exotic dancers, glamorous call girls and prostitutes were part of everyday life. Archer Street, in particular, was a busy haunt for musicians, and at times, the street would be packed with men and women hoping to be picked for the Atlantic run. The lucky ones that did get to go would spend much of their free time in the popular fashion districts of New York, being lured into buying stylish fancy goods, jewellery and colourful American clothes in the latest fabrics, styles and cuts, to perhaps sell back home.

With Soho's risqué credentials, its pubs, clubs and streets inevitably became a ready-made shop floor and hive of black market activities. Many Spivs operated from the area, dealing in everything from diamonds and furs, to paste jewellery and nylons and much sought-after American goods from the returning session musicians.

Proper Gents

This invaluable access to imported fashion meant that the Spivs themselves were among the first to sport the then-fashionable American look, which must have appeared as quite extreme when seen amid the sombreness of wartime Britain.

It was almost as it they modelled themselves on famous Hollywood movie stars, such as James Cagney, George Raft, Alan Ladd and Humphrey Bogart, who were all renowned for portraying gangsters or private detectives, with their bold-striped or check double-breasted suits, trilbies, dark shirts, light ties and two-tone correspondent shoes. One other important signature of the British Spiv was a pencil moustache; this, too, had almost certainly been inspired by some of the great Hollywood movie stars who sported them, like Errol Flynn and Clark Gable.

There was nothing inconspicuous about the way these characters dressed and acted: they were, after all, salesmen who wanted to be noticed, and who would openly flaunt their wares knowing there was little chance of arrest by an overstretched police force. With jewellery on their jacket lapels, rows of watches on their coat linings and pockets full of nylons and cigarettes, the public flocked to them like bees to honey.

When English tailor to the stars Cecil Gee introduced his version of the American look to England in 1946, the style became immensely popular with musicians, showbiz folk, bookmakers and young men who also sought to emulate Hollywood movie stars of the time.

Below: Al Ramsen, *City Across The River*, dir Maxwell Shane, 1949.

Right: Fig 1. Deep red tweed overcoat, 1940s, Dominant, England. White cotton blouse with peplum, red and blue floral print, 1940s, An Auerbach Model, USA. Red rayon skirt with pleated hem, 1940s, Ashionwise, England. Deep red suede peep-toe platform shoes, 1940s, Jack Jacobus CC41, Shaftsbury Avenue, London. Red plastic belt. Blue and yellow plastic stylised medal brooch, 1940s, England. Black leather gloves.

Fig 2. Grey and red windowpane check tweed sports jacket with pleat pocket details, 1940s, Burton Tailoring, Edinburgh. Green cotton waffle embossed shirt, 1940s, Meritus, England. Red rayon tie with black and cream spiral print, 1940s, Tootal Tie, England. Red silk hanky. Grey wool trousers, 1940s, England.

Left: Fig 1. Grey wool birds eye suit, 1940s, CC41, England. Brown cotton spear-point collar shirt, 1940s, Janco Brand, England. Brown and cream bold stripe rayon tie, 1940s, England.

Fig 2. Brown wool herringbone suit, 1950s, England. White cotton shirt, 1950s, England. Green satin chain print tie, 1940s, England. Green wool cardigan, 1950s, Jaeger, England. Brown leather shoes, 1950s, England.

Fig 3. Brown cord bomber jacket, 1940s, England. White and green stripe spear-point shirt, 1940s, Turret Brand CC41, England. Green wool boxing print tie, Tootal, England. Brown wool chalk stripe trousers, 1940s, England.

Fig 4. Green and buff houndstooth check wool sports jacket, 1940s, England. Buff wool sweater, 1940s, England. Yellow paisley print cravat, 1940s, England. Brown gabardine trousers, 1940s, England.

Gee had gained a considerable reputation for selling all the latest off-the-peg styles in menswear at his Whitechapel Road shop in the late 1920s, to which people travelled from all over Britain. In 1932, he moved to the West End and opened his famous Charing Cross Road shop. By the mid 1930s, he had introduced zip-fly openings on men's trousers, and the jacket shirt from America, which buttoned all the way down the front, superseding the old traditional placket-front shirt, which only buttoned half way down its front and had to be pulled on over the head.

The American style became so popular that on Saturdays long queues formed at Gee's shop, and he became known as the 'American Tailor', with customers eager to buy his exciting alternative to the dreary standard issue de-mob suit. Using a basic palette of colours and cloths which included pale blue, American tan, pink and loud chalk stripes, Gee copied the American pattern with both single- and double-breasted suits, which had wide shoulders and draped backs, but with a closer fit than the American original. These he complemented with imported spear-point shirts, Stetson hats, colourful socks, two-tone shoes and hand-painted satin ties, all direct from America. For a little extra money, the ties could be painted with an image from a customer's own photograph. The American look remained a favourite with fashionable young men right through to the mid 1950s, mostly as an alternative to the Teddy Boy style, but Gee stopped selling the look when it became too associated with Soho gangs, Spivs and Drones.

The British movie *Cosh Boy*, 1953, starring young Joan Collins in a very early role, features a gang of violent teenagers who frequent notorious London Spiv haunts dressed in great examples of Gee's American look. The film was banned in Sweden because of its violent content, and the nickname 'cosh boy' was sometimes used by the press when referring to Teddy Boys.

Although Spivs were thought to be mainly from working class backgrounds, they would often refer to themselves as 'proper gents' or gentlemen, and clearly took dress references from affluent city types who used Savile Row tailors.

Wartime rationing meant that suit jackets were cut wshorter and were more fitted, using only the minimum amount of fabric allowed, but adept tailors soon crafted subtle styling details on jackets, such as gauntlet cuffs, half belts, pleated backs, fancy darts and hand-picked stitching – features that spoke volumes to those in the know. Contrasting waistcoats, fancy bowties and loud pattern ties also became fashionable alongside the trend for snap-brim trilbies, Homburg and bowler hats which were *de rigueur*.

Brogue and Oxford toecap shoes in suede also became very popular, even though men who wore suede shoes were considered to be either from low-life circles or even homosexual by correct tailoring standards.

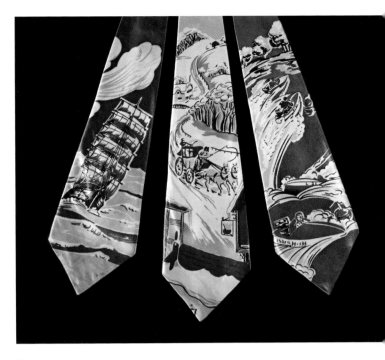

Above: Purple, pink and red galleon print, stage coach print, power boat print ties, 1940s, England. These dead stock 1940s ties were sold at Malcolm McLaren and Vivienne Westwood's shop, Let It Rock, London, in the 1970s.

Left: Brown wool herringbone suit, 1950s, England. White cotton shirt, 1950s, England. Green satin chain print tie, 1940s, England. Green wool cardigan, 1950s, Jaeger, England. Brown leather shoes, 1950s, England.

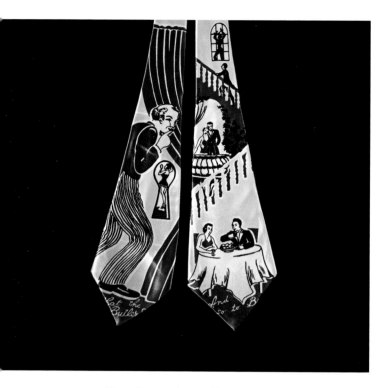

Above: Brown and cream 'What the Butler Saw' print satin tie, 1940s, England. Brown and cream 'And so to Bed' print satin tie, 1940s, England. These dead stock 1940s ties were sold at Malcolm McLaren and Vivienne Westwood's shop, Let It Rock, London, in the 1970s.

Right: Fig 1. Brown fur coat, 1940s, CC41, England. Fern green botany wool top, 1940s, England. Black rayon skirt, 1940s, England. Black lizard skin peep toe platform shoes, 1940s, made in Argentina. Graduated light wood beads, 1940s, England. Floral bakelite belt buckle, 1940s, England.

Fig 2. Brown worsted suit with red windowpane check, 1940s, John Collier, England. White cotton striped spear point collar shirt, 1940s, England. Gilt collar pin. Brown satin hand painted pin-up tie, 1940s, Supreme Tie, England. White silk pocket handkerchief. Silver watch chain. Tan leather shoes, 1940s style, Loakes, England.

Black Market Boogie

Despite the lack of hard cash in circulation there were always a few Spivs with real money who went after hard-to-come-by fabrics, such as silk, cashmere, vicuna and millionaire's gabardine, and then had them hand tailored into their own distinctive style. In comparison with the general issue de-mob clothes of the time, these racketeers must have appeared like the rakish dandies of the eighteenth century, and as such attracted equally glamorous girls to their company. Some Spivs adopted huge personalities to match their clothes, and got up to all sorts of antics, while 'ducking and diving' around seedy city areas avoiding the strong arm of the law. As a consequence, they were constantly being blamed for even basic food shortages, and holding on to contraband goods in order to raise the prices. The police, who were under mounting pressure from the government and public alike to eradicate this growing menace, would make regular raids and arrests of Spivs at well-known underground haunts, such as night clubs and clip joints.

British servicemen returning home from the War were given a full set of civilian clothing to help the transition back into normal life. They were issued with a trilby hat or flat cap, two shirts; a three-piece double-breasted suit in grey, brown or navy-blue pin-striped wool or a single-breasted jacket and flannel trousers; a tie; stout shoes and a raincoat, all of good quality, although in fashion terms, quite dated. So much so that some servicemen refused to wear the clothes they had been given, because they said they made them look like old-style gangsters, and instead would happily sell their clothes to eager Spivs who always had cash and customers waiting for them.

The Spivs' black-market exploits became legendary and were regularly caricatured by the famous music hall comedians of the time, such as Arthur English, Sid Field and Max Miller. Arthur English was famous for his dodgy antics and for wearing a huge, floral kipper tie right down to his knees. Field actually played a long-running stage character called Slasher Green, where he not only mimicked a Spiv's behaviour, but dressed from head to toe in highly exaggerated Spiv-style clothes; he also appeared in the 1946 hit film *London Town*. Cheeky Chappie Max Miller also had an entire wardrobe of eccentric stage outfits, which were his trademark. In clothes tailored from colourful furnishing fabric in bright floral prints, he clearly took influence from European white-faced clowns with his tight fitting jackets and huge plus-fours, garishly patterned ties, snap-brim trilbies and two-tone correspondent shoes. Miller was most famous for his blue humour routines, which were laden with subtle innuendo and double entendre: *'I know exactly what you're saying. You're saying to yourselves, "Why is he dressed like that?" I'll tell you why I'm dressed like this. I'm a commercial traveller and I'm ready for bed!' (Max Miller).*

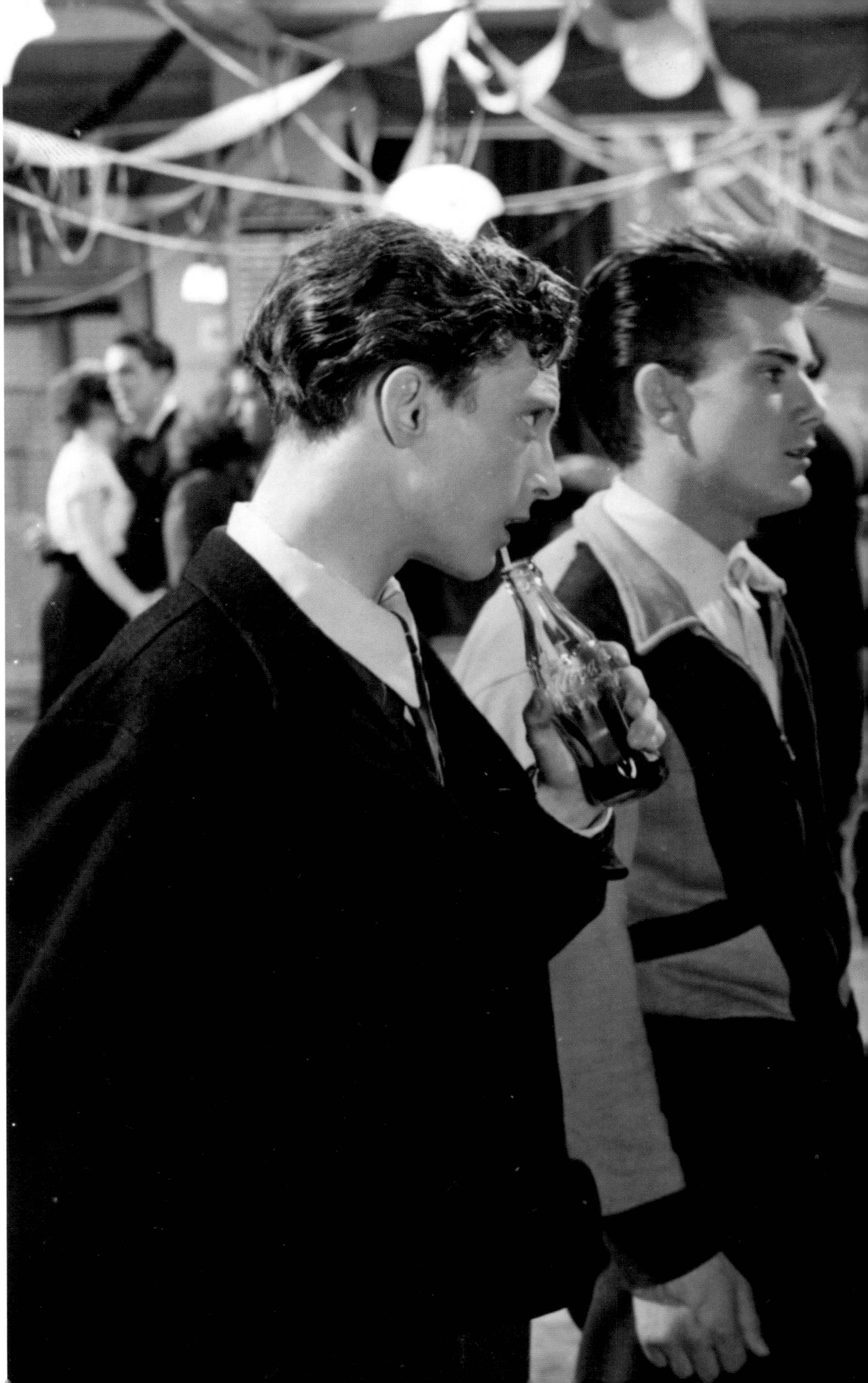

Right: *Cosh Boy*, dir Lewis Gilbert, 1953.

Above: Joan Collins and James Kenney, *Cosh Boy*, dir Lewis Gilbert, 1953.

Right: Fig 1 Grey worsted skirt suit, 1940s, England. Yellow wool shawl collar sweater, 1940s, England. Black leather platform sole court shoes with perforated bow detail, 1940s, Char:Min CC41, England. Perspex floral brooch, 1940s, England.

Fig 2. Navy worsted stripe suit, 1940s, Mathis, Portland Oregon. White spear point collar shirt, 1940s, England. Red and silver grey stripe tie with hairpin print, 1940s, England. Gilt sword tie clip, 1940s, England. Black leather Oxford toe cap shoes, 1940s, England. Red silk pocket hanky.

Left: Fig 1. Grey worsted suit, 1940s, Burton's The Tailor, England. Pale blue spear-point collar shirt, 1940s, England. Blue satin and silver striped tie, 1940s, England. Blue silk pocket handkerchief. Black leather toecap shoes, 1940s, England.

Fig 2. White linen dress with navy blue floral and window print, 1940s, Peggy Page CC41, England. Navy leather shoes with white golf tongue detail, 1940s, Holmes, Norwich. Gold locket bracelet.

Right: Grey wool birds eye suit, 1940s, CC41, England. Brown cotton spear-point collar shirt, 1940s, Janco Brand, England. Brown and cream bold stripe rayon tie, 1940s, England.

Passing Clouds

Although Spivs were very much in the public eye during the 1940s, in reality there were only ever a few in existence, and consequently there is very little visual documentation of the genuine article other than those portrayed in films such as *Waterloo Road*, 1945, *Appointment with Crime*, 1946, *Brighton Rock*, 1947, *It Always Rains on Sunday*, 1947, and *Good-Time Girl*, 1948, among others. Nevertheless, their mythological influence on men's fashion at the time was very important.

The era of the Spiv finally passed with the end of rationing, and most moved on to using their entrepreneurial skills in other prospering trades, such as bankrupt stock and used cars. By the mid 1950s that famous look, that had once appeared so outrageous and colourful on the grey British wartime streets, was no more than a fond memory.

Right: Fig 1. Grey chalk stripe three-piece suit, 1947, F J Soulsby, Blackpool. White and beige and cream stripe spear-point collar shirt, 1940s, England. Silver collar pin, Navy, silver and red stylised dragons flame print tie, 1940s, England. Diamante and paste costume jewelry, 1940s, England. Red silk paisley print pocket handkerchief. Black and white leather two-tone shoes, 1940s style, England.

Fig 2. Black wool sweater with cream sawfish front panel, 1940s, England. Black rayon skirt with button detail on pockets, Stylemaster, 1940s, England. Black leather high heel platform peep toe shoes, 1940s, Foot Delight Los Angeles. Clear Perspex bangle, 1940s, England.

Fig 3. Chocolate brown crepe dress with ochre rococo collar and belt trim, 1940s, England. Oval Perspex brooch with inset crinoline lady, 1940s, England. Cream nu-buck lace up shoes with brogue detail and brown leather toe caps, 1940s, Fashioncraft CC41, England.

Fig 4. Cream and grey check wool coat with black cord collar and cuffs, 1940s, England. Black wool sweater with silver beaded applique, 1940s, England. Black gabardine skirt, 1940s, England. Black leather high heel court shoes, 1940s, Marlone, England.

Above: British Spiv selling black market brooches and a camera, London, 1945.

Left: A rare, full size, three-piece patchwork tailor's apprentice suit, c.1946-49, England. These suits were usually constructed in ½ scale by tailor's apprentices from cutting room floor scraps, and no piece of cloth or button is the same. The finished suits would take pride of place in the tailor's shop window displaying the skill of their staff. White cotton spear point collar shirt, 1940s, England. Gilt collar pin. Green, red and cream striped tie with abstract brush strokes, 1940s, England. Brown leather and suede two-tone shoes, 1940s style, F Funaro, Italy.

Right: 1. Brown felt Homberg hat, 1940s, England.

2. Silver belly felt Homberg hat, 1940s, England.

3. Brown felt trilby hat, 1940s, England.

Opposite: The Original Spiv, 26th June 1952.

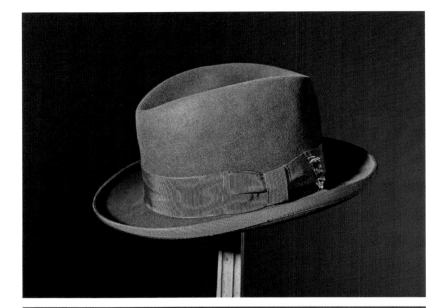

PUTTING ON THE STYLE

TEDDY BOYS & GIRLS

LATE 1940s – LATE 1950s

"He may be the modern version of the masher. Or he may be part of a springing new crop of male wallflowers. Sometimes he is the first with the latest style. Sometimes he is a slavish follower, anxious to wear the uniform of the gang. Wherever he is found, whoever he is, the wearer of the Teddy Boy suit is proclaiming his masculinity."

Norman Phillips, *Illustrated Magazine*, 1955.

It is noted in the historical ledgers of Savile Row that on 17th January 1942, at the height of wartime rationing, a young Scottish fusilier took delivery of a very lavish Edwardian-style suit from a Conduit Street tailor. He had chosen to wear the suit as a protest against wartime austerity. The fusilier's actions could be deciphered as the ultimate in snobbery, or at the very least an act of supreme decadence. However, the tailors of Savile Row must have been used to this kind of behaviour from generation after generation of upper-class dandies, rich gentry, eccentric young bucks and royalty, who made similarly unconventional requests during times of conflict.

The New Edwardian Look

For centuries, Savile Row tailors have considered themselves world leaders in men's fashion and the height of good taste, seeking only to provide the finest in tradition and quality to their esteemed customers. So cutting a suit in the style of the late Edward VII would merely have been a matter of carrying on tradition – even though the cut of the fusilier's suit was probably modified from the original pattern and brought up to date. New designs and patterns take a long time to refine in Savile Row and it was not until 1950, a year after clothes rationing had ended, that several tailors decided to introduce the 'New Edwardian' look into their pattern books.

In 1947, they had been asked by the British Menswear Association to produce a new cut that was different to the old de-mob style, but after three years of refinement they had failed to find an alternative that met with approval.

However, one tailor observed that several ex-Guards officer customers had been ordering Edwardian 'mashers' style suits for some years (and these chaps had almost certainly taken inspiration from the Scottish fusilier from 1942). The New Edwardian look had also been seen in stylish homosexual circles, championed by society photographer and designer Cecil Beaton and the couturier Bunny Roger. With this in mind, the Savile Row tailors decided to exhibit the style at a private show, being modelled by Beaton, Roger and fashion photographer Norman Parkinson. The new line of suit consisted of a long, slightly flared jacket with a slim waist, natural shoulders, a velvet collar and cuffs and narrow-fitting tapered trousers with turn-ups. The whole ensemble was coordinated with a brightly patterned waistcoat.

The show was a success, and an adaptation of the 'New Mayfair Edwardian Look' (as it also became known) was quickly taken up by the retail menswear trade. Clothing manufacturers had invested heavily in new machinery after the War, and much to the horror and surprise of the Savile Row brigade, almost any design could now be copied quite cheaply and produced in quantity virtually overnight.

Previous page: *The Violent Playground*, dir Basil Deardon, 1958.

Right: Fig 1. Greige and cream fleck check worsted New Edwardian early 1950s style suit, A Golberg, 1980s reproduction, England. Grey wool double-breasted waistcoat, 1940s, Akco Tailored Dresswear, England. Grey cotton shirt, 1950s, Sata-Piata. Red and navy self-striped silk tie, 1950s, England.

Fig 2. Grey Prince of Wales check with red over-check New Edwardian style jacket, early 1950s, The West End Clothiers, Leicester. Black double-breasted wool waistcoat, 1940s, England. Grey herringbone trousers, 1950s, England. White cotton shirt, 1950s, England. Red and dark red stripe silk tie, 1950s, England.

Above: Hugh O'Brian, *The Life and Legend of Wyatt Earp*, 1955.

Right: Fig 1. Salmon pink wool drape coat with Western style pockets, link button and black velvet trim, 1950s, England. Beige grosgrain waistcoat, 1950s, England. White cotton shirt, 1950s, England. Yellow ochre gambler bowtie with diamante trim, 1950s, USA. Black wool drainpipe trousers, 1950s, England.

Fig 2. Taupe wool jacket with multi button detail, 1940s, England. White cotton roll-collar shirt, 1950s, England. Black velvet ribbon. Basalt and ivory plastic cameo brooch, 1950s, England. Black gabardine skirt, 1940s, England.

Teddy Boys

There had been a growing demand for alternatives to the de-mob suit from young men since clothes rationing had finished, and by early 1952 the cash tills of suburban menswear shops were ringing with sales to newly affluent teenagers who had begun to buy the high-street version of the New Edwardian look. By 1953, the nickname 'Teddy Boy' was being bandied about to describe boys who wore the look, who mostly originated from traditional, die-hard, working-class areas of London, such as Hackney, Tottenham, Shepherd's Bush and particularly Elephant and Castle (which is considered by most to be the place where the style first appeared). Because many people considered the Edwardian look as an anti-social form of dress, the boys were victimised by the press, police and outraged adults.

Savile Row, of course, wanted no association with bad press and several exclusive tailors dropped the New Edwardian look like a hot potato, although Beaton and his cronies continued to sport the style for several more years, and Bunny Roger never stopped wearing the look until his death in 1997 at the age of 85.

What the original Teddy Boys chose to wear was actually quite close in appearance to the Savile Row model, but with a less fitted, slightly longer jacket and tighter leg trousers. And their choice of fabrics – predominantly houndstooth and Prince-of-Wales check – were certainly very similar at the outset. Velvet collars were considered a bit affected at first, but very soon kids with a little more money and individuality began to experiment with these subtle details that added to the entire look and made it their own.

The most extroverted Teddy Boys started to emulate their B-movie Western heroes, such as the frock-coated gamblers, who wore fancy waistcoats and bootlace ties, and the legendary Wyatt Earp, whose own style of bowtie became a trend. Clark Gable, who played Rhett Butler in *Gone with the Wind*, must have been an inspirational figure in his Victorian frock-coat in much the same way that wartime Spivs would have been influenced by gangster movies of the 1930s and 1940s. In fact, the Spivs themselves probably had quite an influence on the way the Teds dressed, with their outlandish suit fabrics, loud ties and cocky behaviour. Although long draped zoot suits were quite rare in Britain, they were seen around dance halls just after the War, having been introduced by American servicemen.

Cecil Gee's Charing Cross Road shop, which had specialised in the American look since 1946, also supplied many early Teds with important accessories, like crepe-soled shoes, flex-roll shirts and Wyatt Earp ties direct from America. Although the American look remained popular with many young men as a fashionable alternative to the Teddy Boy style until the mid 1950s, to most Teds it was not even a contender.

Drapes

The long 'drape' jacket, as it was generally known, refers to the back of the jacket, which was cut in one piece, fully draped with no vents and varied in length from fingertip to knee-skimming. Solid colour fabrics followed check weaves, and these were very popular in black, maroon or navy. Most featured a velvet collar, cuffs, buttons and cowboy-style curved jetted pockets, some with arrowhead details. Wide-notch lapels or a shawl collar with a low-fastening, single-link button were both acceptable, but as many as six buttons were noted. Shirts were just as important in the Teds' overall appearance, and one style that early Teds particularly favoured was called 'Mr B' – a cutaway collar shirt designed by popular Jazz trumpeter Billy Eckstine (*see Chapter One*).

From these standard styles, many individual variations appeared. Exactly where the use of bright colours came from is not certain, but probably preceded fierce competition at the growing number of organised 'Best Dressed Ted' competitions that occurred during 1954 around London's Mecca ballrooms. Teddy Boys formed a pretty menacing silhouette with their long jackets, tight drainpipe trousers and heavy American style crepe-soled shoes, all topped off with a huge Brylcreem or Vaseline quiff hairdo.

Many boys who were banned from youth clubs formed street corner gangs, and looked for trouble wherever they went. Racist attacks, muggings, street fights with rival gangs, and fights at dances over girls occurred on a regular basis. The press had a field day reporting on the latest campaign of terror supposedly perpetrated by Teds. It is hard to know how much truth there was in the stories of violence, but they fuelled the myth that, although many boys were innocent, anyone wearing a drape was labelled a 'juvenile delinquent'.

Certainly there were some hard cases around. One particularly heavy gang, who considered themselves 'the business', were known to have worn bright-red hunting-style coats on their sorties, and one member was said to have even blown on a hunting horn to announce the gang's presence. Teds carried a number of weapons, such as bike chains, coshes, knuckle-dusters and cut-throat razors, but none was more popular than the flick knife, or 'shiv', as it was commonly known. Sticking the nut on your rival was also a popular macho act, and in order to counter this, boys would sew fishhooks or razor blades on the backs of their lapels for defence, as the assailant would usually grab the lapels to ensure no escape was made by the victim.

The general public had every reason to be worried by the gangs. Mounting pressure was put upon the police to clean up the streets as, by 1955, it was estimated that over 10,000 Teds were based in London alone. How many were actually true Teddy Boys is debatable.

Above: Chuck Day, Hugh Finnegan and Merv, Jeromes Studios, Portsmouth, October 1956, Courtesy Hugh Finnegan.

Left: Fig 1. Black jacket with white wire mesh print and velvet trim, 1950s, Matita, England. White cotton roll-collar shirt, 1950s, England. Beige and ivory glass cameo brooch, 1950s, England. Black wool skirt, 1950s, England. Black leather crepe-soled loafers with white stitching, 1950s, Kiltie by Norvic, England.

Fig 2. Grey wool Prince of Wales check 1950s Edwardian style drape suit with black velvet trim, 1980s reproduction, D&G Tailors, Ingrebourne. Black wool waistcoat, 1950s, England. White cotton shirt, 1950s, England. Black and grey striped silk tie, 1950s, England. Black leather 1950s style crepe-soled shoes, 1970s reproduction, England.

Every sub-culture spawns copy-cats and even by this time most kids could not afford a proper Ted suit, which handmade would cost between £15 and £20 for a two- or three-piece suit. To save money but still give the impression of wearing a waistcoat, some kids would have a 4- to 6-inch wide waistband sewn on their trousers. One way of achieving the look without having a drape tailor-made was to buy a second-hand adult's jacket, several sizes too big, and then get someone handy with a needle and thread to take it in and shorten the sleeves. Kids would also buy a cheap pair of black or blue jeans, borrow a pair of Dad's work boots or heavy Oxford toecap shoes, pull on an old-school V-neck tank top or cardigan, and buy, or steal, a Slim-Jim tie from Woolworths to complete the outfit. Thousands of impressionable but poor young boys took this route, and under a cover of darkness would assume the familiar-silhouetted identity of regal Teddy Boys.

> 'Ed the Ted – When the Ted-thing became all the rage Edward signed up for the duration, and joined the Teddy-boy wolf cubs, or whatever they're called, and later graduated through the Ted high school up the Harrow road to the full-fledged Teddy-boy condition – slit eyes, and cosh, and words of one syllable, and dirty finger-nails and all – and left his broken-hearted Mum and Dad, who gave three rousing cheers, and emigrated down to Bermondsey, to join a gang.'

Absolute Beginners *by Colin MacInnes 1959.*

The seminal cult novel *Absolute Beginners*, set in London's Soho in 1958, gives the reader a graphic account of all the popular sub-cultural fashions of the time, each illustrated through its many colourful characters. The book gives us a vivid picture of what life must have been like for many frustrated teenagers growing up in post-war England.

Teds would hang out in pool rooms or down at the local amusement arcades, playing the latest pinball machines. Saturday mornings were taken up with a visit to the barbers and buying clothes and records, football in the afternoon and up to the local Mecca ballroom at night. The boys would never go out for the evening unless they looked immaculate, for they knew there was fierce competition between peer groups. They also had to run the gauntlet of the girls who would be waiting at the dance, as the girls always seemed to know which boys had spent the most on their outfit that week. In a display of style, lots of time was spent combing their hair and getting the quiff just right. Cool guys always did it in front of the girls and wherever there was an audience, mirror or shop-window reflection.

Although Teddy Boys were usually in the press for causing trouble, a piece in a 1954 *Picture Post* magazine,

Above: L-R Albie Deacon, Johnnie Moore, Graham Butcher, Brian Frost, Hugh Finnegan and Eugeen Finnegan. Jeromes Studios, Portsmouth, August 1956. Courtesy Hugh Finnegan.

then the UK's equivalent of America's *Life* magazine, featured quite an objective article entitled: 'The truth about the "Teddy Boys" and the "Teddy Girls"', which was written by a psychiatrist. His overall view of this popular cult was that in the main the boys were just adolescents having to deal with the everyday trials of becoming adults. And he summarised, '*They are like an army that needs gorgeous uniforms, and heroic border incidents – because it has never fought a real campaign. The Edwardian clothes are at once a shield against the world and a shield to hide inner vulnerability.*' This well-observed quote could apply to many of the other sub-cultures featured in this book.

Even though the main focus of the press always seemed to target Teddy Boys, a lot of girls also wore the look, and girl gangs were known to exist. In fact, just a year later, in 1955, a startling series of black-and-white photos featuring an extraordinary gang of working class teenage Teddy Girls also appeared in *Picture Post* magazine. The piece, entitled 'What's wrong with Teddy Girls?', was shot by the then-budding film director Ken Russell. Posed by Russell on a London bombsite, these androgynous teenage girls display an attitude that screams of Teddy Boy bravado and aggression, and yet the article points out that 'the girls, also known as Judies, all have good jobs, are very proud of their clothes and just see their look as just an alternative fashion'.

Right: Fig 1. Black wool suit jacket, 1940s, England. Red wool sweater, 1950s, England. Red silk neck scarf. Blue denim jeans, 1950s, Selrig, England. Navy leather slip-on shoes, 1950s, Moccasin, England.

Fig 2. Black wool suit jacket, 1940s, England. Silver and pearl floral brooch, 1950s, England. Deep pink wool sweater, 1950s, Miladi-Anne, England. Red silk paisley neck scarf. Blue denim jeans, 1950s, Selrig, England. Black leather crepe-soled loafers with white stitching, 1950s, Kiltie by Norvic, England.

Fig 3. Black wool suit jacket, 1940s, England. Red wool sweater, 1950s, Berketex, England. Red cotton paisley neck scarf. Blue denim jeans, 1950s, Tek-Sak, England. Black mesh pumps with white rubber soles, 1950s, England.

Fig 4. Black and buttermilk striped viscose jacket, 1940s, England. Buttermilk cotton froll-neck blouse, 1950s, Red Girl, England. Black silk ribbon. Black basalt and ivory plastic cameo brooch, 1950s, England. Black denim jeans, 1950s, Lybro, England. Black leather strappy sandals, 1950s, England.

Fig 5. Black wool suit jacket, 1940s, England. Red wool sweater, 1950s, Jersyvic, England. Red silk neck scarf. Blue denim jeans, 1950s, Real Virginian, England. Black canvas plimsolls.

Left: Teddy Girl Jeanie Rayner, photo Ken Russell, North Kensington, London 1955.

Right: Fig 1. Red wool 1950s style drape coat with velvet trim, 1970s reproduction, Dave Wax, London. White cotton shirt, 1950s, England. Black satin Wyatt Earp bowtie, 1970s reproduction, USA. Black wool drainpipe trousers, 1950s, England. Fluorescent green socks. Black leather 1950s style crepe-soled shoes, 1970s reproduction, England.

Fig 2. Black and white houndstooth drape coat with velvet trim, late 1950s, Rosemans Tailoring, England. Black grosgrain waistcoat, 1950s, England. White cotton shirt, 1950s, England. White polyester tie with red diamond motif, 1950s, Distinctive Ties, England. Black wool drainpipe trousers, 1950s, England. Pink fluorescent socks. Pink suede 1950s style crepe-soled shoes, 1970s reproduction, England.

Fig 3. Red wool 1950s style drape coat with velvet trim, 1970s reproduction, England. Black and yellow waffle weave waistcoat, 1950s, England. White cotton shirt, 1950s, England. Black Petersham ribbon bowtie. Black wool drainpipe trousers, 1950s, England. Ice blue fluorescent socks. Blue suede 1950s style crepe-soled shoes, 1970s reproduction, England.

Left: Fig 1. Red wool suit jacket, 1940s, England. Pink nylon blouse with black sparkly collar, 1950s, England. Wedgewood blue ceramic cameo, 1950s, England. Maroon denim jeans, 1950s, England.

Fig 2. Black wool jacket, 1950s, Town & Country, Coronado. White nylon top with red lurex stripes, 1950s, England. Red wool plaid trousers, 1950s England. Black canvas slip-on plimsolls.

Fig 3. Grey and black houndstooth 1950s style drape jacket, 1980s reproduction. Red and grey cotton check shirt, 1950s, Measurmade, England. Black wool trousers, 1950s, England. Red nylon socks. Blue suede 1950s style side buckle crepe-soled shoes, 1970s reproduction, England.

Fig 4. Green embossed wool jacket, 1950s, Matita, England. Pressed tin Rosemary Clooney fan brooch, 1950s, USA. White roll-collar shirt with green and black playing card symbols, 1950s, England. Black plastic belt. Black wool straight skirt, 1950s, England.

Right: Teddy Girls at Battersea Funfair, 1956.

Left: Fig 1. White cotton sun dress and jacket with a black palettes and abstract paint splash print, 1950s, Holeproof, New Zealand. Black PVC belt.

Fig 2. Duck egg blue twill suit, 1950s, Hollywood Clothes, Hirsch & Price, San Francisco. Black rayon shirt, 1950s, Water Lane, England.

Right: Fig 1. Powder blue and cream striped shirt-jac, 1950s, Measurmade, England. Cream silk opera scarf, 1950s, England. Blue wool peg top trousers, 1950s, England.

Fig 2. Yellow embossed cotton blouson jacket, 1950s, Le Roi of Piccadilly Sports Model, England. Tan, blue, black and yellow abstract brick print cotton shirt, 1950s, England. Blue and ginger flecked peg top trousers, 1950s, England.

Fig 3. Pale blue and black dogtooth woven cotton blouson jacket, 1950s, Porin Paitatekdas Oy, Finland. White viscose shirt with musical instrument and dancers print, 1950s, Jewel, England. Black peg top trousers, 1950s, England.

The radical new style they were wearing was clearly derived from populist Edwardian fashions, which were also being reworked by mainstream women's wear designers. Generally, girls earned less than boys, and although a few of the girls in Russell's photos are wearing tailored drape coats similar to their Teddy Boy boyfriends over tight hobble skirts, most of the other girls are pictured wearing second-hand black jackets that would have been the height of middle-class fashion almost a decade earlier. Their jackets have perhaps come from their mothers' wardrobes, or more likely quality cast-offs from society ladies found quite cheaply in rummage sales, second-hand shops and on market barrows. The look may appear understated compared with a full drape jacket of the same period, but it actually represents an equally rebellious statement when worn in this way. Even though wartime rationing had only just finished, wearing second-hand, used clothes or hand-me-downs was still frowned upon by all classes of society, and these remarkable images were possibly the first proper documentation of not only a post-War English girl gang but also of teenage boys and girls wearing second-hand clothes as a street style.

In retrospect, you can really see the influence of Edwardian hunting clothes in the way the girls styled themselves, with their high-necked blouses, chiffon scarves, ribbon ties and antique-style cameo brooches in place of a hunting stock. Interestingly, they too wore shirts with deep-rolled cutaway collars similar to the boys.

It was also on market stalls and barrows where the girls and boys would have been introduced to the latest teenage craze of 'American-style' denim jeans.

The new slim-fit cut of jeans was generally worn cropped at calf length by girls and rolled with a deep turn-up. Navy-blue denim with white stitching and black cotton with green stitching were most popular, but before long, fine grey and black stripes similar to banker's formal morning trousers became popular and, teamed with cheap flat black velveteen sneakers or pumps, gave the girls a tough, boyish look, unlike any teenage girls' fashion seen before in the UK. This was interpreted as yet another affront to grown-ups and authority.

Authentic American jeans were not readily available in the UK in the mid 1950s, and as a result enterprising English companies, such as Lee Cooper, Westcott, Lybro and Jewel began churning out cheap inferior copies of American jeans to cater for this new, growing youth market. These thin, cotton, empire-made jeans were nothing like the heavy, 14oz denim used by American jean manufacturers, and they invariably didn't retain their looks for more than a few washes; however, they were cheap enough for kids to replace them on a regular basis.

Within a short time these much sought-after jeans would be available in a variety of colours such as ice blue, maroon and iridescent bronze, gold or green, and they continued to be popular with all kinds of teenagers well into the early 1960s. Like their American cousins, many English girls took to wearing circular skirts with masses of petticoats that were perfect for dancing in.

Let It Rock

The thing that attracted kids to become Teddy Boys and Teddy Girls more than anything else was the music, and by 1955 rock 'n' roll was taking the UK by storm. Teds lived and breathed rock 'n' roll, buying records obsessively. When Bill Haley's famous song 'Rock Around the Clock' was used as a soundtrack to the film *Blackboard Jungle*, Teds queued for hours to see the film, and once the music started there was wild dancing in the aisles. When the management threatened to stop the film, kids were incensed; seats were slashed with flick knives, torn from their fixings and hurled at the screen. Many cinemas were wrecked in the film's wake. Successive tours by rock 'n' roll stars such as Bill Haley, Little Richard, Jerry Lee Lewis and Chuck Berry were massive sell-outs and promoters could not believe their luck; but as each concert was played, the frenzied Teds ran rampage and destroyed the venue, causing an abrupt and bloody end to the proceedings. For several months it seemed as if everything was out of control, and the situation got even worse when Teds took to the streets. Pockets of rioting teenagers sprang up everywhere and the police had to take drastic measures, arresting hundreds before calm prevailed.

Right: Fig 1. White cotton blouse with red stripes and spots, 1950s, Red Girl, England. Black cotton skirt with jazz posters and music print, 1950s, England. Red patent stiletto shoes with tartan inserts, 1950s, England.

Fig 2. Salmon pink cotton blouse, 1950s, England. Royal blue cotton skirt with jive dancers on records, 1950s, England. Pink PVC belt. Salmon pink leather court shoes, 1950s, England.

Fig 3. Yellow cotton blouse, 1950s, Trutex, England. Black cotton skirt with film star photo prints and hand painted scenes, 1950s, England. Black leather court shoes, 1950s, England.

Many original Teds would become disheartened as they saw all this trouble leading to the end of a fabulous dream, and by 1956 many had given up the look entirely. For some time, their tough image had attracted troublemakers and the wrong sort, and it seemed like every teenage boy who had a DA ('duck's arse') or Tony Curtis hairstyle was now being labelled a Teddy Boy and a delinquent by the general public. In reality, the true Teds' incredible passion for the music, wearing the clothes and having fun was forever being dampened by the police, and would never be the same again.

Teddy Boys would again hit the headlines in 1958 as they became involved in the nasty race riots around London's Notting Hill, which at that time was predominantly a poor black area and hotbed of racial tension. White extremists targeted the area and demanded that the recent influx of immigrant West Indians be driven out of the country, because they felt they were taking white folks' jobs and causing unemployment. Brutal attacks and the burning of property by hundreds of roaming gangs were the worst the country had seen in over ten years.

By the close of the 1950s, most Teds had lost their way and become outmoded as a new type of clothes fanatic was starting to replace them. These kids, who dressed in the latest cool Italian style and listened to Modern Jazz, were to pave the way for an even bigger movement in the 1960s, that of the 'Mod'.

Right: Fig 1.White embossed cotton dress with pink flower and green polygon print, 1950s, England. Pale pink teddy bear jacket, 1950s, USA. White PVC belt. Cream leather court shoes, 1950s, England.

Fig 2. Blue worsted suit with link buttons, 1950s, England. Navy and white fleck woven rayon shirt, 1950s, Wensdale, London. Black leather 1950s style crepe-soled shoes, 1970s reproduction, England.

Fig 3. Taupe gabardine jacket with link buttons, 1950s, American Tailor, Hong Kong. Pink and taupe woven paisley waistcoat, 1950s, England. White cotton shirt, 1950s, Jewel, England. Black wool peg top trousers, 1950s, England. Grey suede crepe-soled shoes, 1950s, Playboy by Hutton, Northampton.

Fig 4. Yellow embossed cotton dress with black abstract floral print, 1950s, Selcourt, South Africa. Cream virgin wool bolero jacket with Eiffel Tower and champagne applique, 1950s, Helen Harper, USA. Black suede kitten heel shoes with patent trim, 1950s, England.

Left: Fig 1. Royal blue sweater with pale blue and white yolk, 1950s, Sheik, England. White cut-away collar shirt, 1950s, Juwel, Germany. Black flannel 1950s style peg top trousers with silver and red flecks, 1980s, Johnsons, London. Black leather crepe-soled shoes, 1950s, Playboy by Hutton, Northampton.

Fig 2. Royal blue cotton cardigan with grey front panels, 1950s, L Tricot de Qualite, Paris. Cream and gold fleck woven cotton shirt, 1950s, Schenley of California. Grey worsted peg top trousers, 1950s, England. Black leather slip-on crepe-soled shoes, 1950s, England.

Fig 3. Royal blue cotton cardigan with grey yolk, 1950s, England. Red cotton shirt, 1950s, Famella, England. Navy fleck wool trousers, 1950s, England. Black leather crepe-soled shoes with brogue top and side buckle, 1950s, 'Silver Leaf' American Italian Styled by Piago, England.

Right: Window shopping at Williams American style clothing, Charing Cross Road, 1951.

Right: Fig 1. Black wool blazer with silver lurex thread, 1950s, England. White polished cotton diamond pattern shirt, 1950s, Daylin, England. Red tartan bowtie, 1950s, USA. Black gabardine trousers, 1950s, England.

Fig 2. Red and black leopard print fake fur coat, 1950s, Vinmont, England. Silver and grey lurex wired bustier, 1950s, England. Black crepe hobble skirt with peplum, 1950s, USA.

Fig 3. Gold and black striped lurex blazer with cream and silver sequin applique, 1950s, England. Black cotton shirt, 1950s, England. Silver cow skull bolo bootlace tie, 1950s, England.

4

THE WILD ONES

BIKERS, ROCKERS & OUTLAWS

MID 1940s – LATE 1960s

"We wanna be free! We wanna be free to do what we wanna do. We wanna be free to ride. We wanna be free to ride our machines without being hassled by The Man! And we wanna get loaded. And we wanna have a good time. And that's what we're gonna do. We are gonna have a good time...We are gonna have a party."

Heavenly Blues, (Peter Fonda) *The Wild Angels*, 1966.

During the 1930s and 1940s, American motorcycle clubs were regularly promoted as popular groups of young people enjoying a healthy activity. That was until 4 July 1947, when some 4,000 motorcycle enthusiasts roared into the small Californian town of Hollister for the annual racing and hill-climbing event organised by the AMA (American Motorcycle Association). The town's seven-man police force watched in terror as the crowds, crazed with alcohol, wreaked havoc over three days and nights. Illegal drag races took place in the main streets, red lights were ignored, bikers drove into bars, smashed windows, fights and brawling broke out, and the streets were awash with urine, beer bottles and rubbish. Almost 50 bikers were put in jail and 60 people were injured. Finally the state troopers were called in to clear the town.

Later the same month, *Life* magazine published an article about the event entitled 'Cyclist's Holiday: He and Friends Terrorize Town', featuring a full-page photograph of one very drunken, nameless Hollister motorcyclist, slouched astride his Harley Davidson motorbike, surrounded by empty beer bottles and detritus. The image shocked a great many *Life* readers.

The photo is now thought to have been staged by the reporter, as another unpublished photo has recently been discovered showing the same young man, now named as Eddie Davenport, on the same bike but in a different pose, wearing a jacket with the words 'Tulare Raiders MC' surrounding a winged skull motif and with the name 'Dave' beneath it. The supposition now is that the jacket belonged to someone else and was borrowed for the photo.

What is clear, though, is that Eddie, or Dave, was more than likely an ex-serviceman, for he is wearing what looks like a naval deck jacket, baseball cap, motorcycle engineer boots, khaki shirt and drill pants.

No doubt many young men up and down the country who had just returned from military service only to find a jobless, no-hope future related to this powerful image. The reality of war had given some, at least, a taste for living on the edge, where adrenalin was an ultimate high and death just another wild throw of the dice. These fearless guys, who were fiercely patriotic, had been to hell and back and were now determined to have a good time. Two months later, on Labor Day, Riverside California fell victim to the same nightmare as Hollister, but this time there were over 6,000 bikers present and one person died.

So these dramatic scenes of lawlessness, which to the bikers had started out as a bit of harmless fun and a release of post-War tension, now shook the foundations of society and led to the police banning any such future events. Roving motorcycle gangs were also banned from the AMA in an attempt to protect the reputation of its more civilised members. Outraged gang members interpreted the ban as deliberate victimisation, marking them as social outcasts, and so some vowed that lawlessness would now become a total lifestyle, enjoyed by a select few of the most notorious outlaws the world had ever seen.

Previous page: The Black Rebels Motorcycle Club and the Beetles standoff, *The Wild One*, dir Lásló Benedek, 1953.

Left: Fig 5. Black leather cross zip biker jacket, 1950s Perfecto Style, USA. White cotton T-shirt with black neckband. Black leather gauntlets 1950s, England. Levi's 501 Jeans, USA. Black leather flying boots, 1950s, England.

Deep turn-ups seen on jeans in the 1940s and 1950s may appear to be a fashion, but they had a more practical reason. Prior to the development of pre-shrunk denim in the early 1960s, kids would have to buy their jeans at least a size too big in the waist and with extra-long legs, to allow for shrinkage with each wash.

Above: Eddie Davenport, Hollister, 4th July 1947.

Right: Black leather work jacket, 1940s, England. Black and grey striped cotton roll-neck. Alloy grinders goggles, Kwikfit, 1950s, England. Black leather army belt, 1950s, England. Khaki army chinos, 1950s, England. Black leather work boots, 1950s, England.

On 17th March 1948, the first chapter of the Hells Angels Motorcycle Club, 'Berdoo', was officially inaugurated, based in San Bernardino California. Its original members were said to have come from a squadron of fearless pilots, bombardiers and gunners who flew B-17s during the Second World War and adorned the fuselages of their bombers with the name 'Hells Angels'. The Angels' volatile reputation preceded them with other clubs wherever they went. One of their main rival clubs was The Outlaws, notoriously America's oldest biker club, formed in 1935 at McCook, Illinois, a suburb of Chicago.

In 1953, a low-budget outlaw biker movie called *The Wild One*, directed by László Benedek, was released. The story was loosely based on the events that had taken place in Hollister six years earlier, and starred teen idol Marlon Brando as Johnny, a smug outlaw biker whose leather-jacketed gang, the Black Rebels Motorcycle Club, terrorise the inhabitants of a small US town, ironically called 'Wrightsville', for no apparent reason other than to have fun. Soon a rival gang, the Beetles, led by Chino (Lee Marvin), rolls into town looking for trouble. Marvin wore an iconic striped T-shirt and an early example of a cut-off leather jacket. In one of the film's most memorable scenes, Johnny leans on the jukebox, drinking beer, when a girl says to him, *'Hey, Johnny, What are you rebelling against?'* After a brief pause Johnny casually comes back with, *'What've you got?'*

Johnny's brooding and yet flippant attitude typified the mood of so many misunderstood youngsters, and the film attained cult status because it actually confirmed the way kids felt. Sales of black leather jackets and motorcycles rocketed across the United States, and some eastern American states would not even allow denim jeans to be worn in high schools, such was the impact of *The Wild One* on teenage culture at the time. Due to the film's controversial nature it was, however, banned in numerous countries in the years following its release; even in America it was feared as a potential cause for riots, and in Britain the film's anti-social threat was taken so seriously that the authorities barred public screenings until 1968, some 14 years after its release.

After seeing the movie, Frank Sadilek, president of the San Francisco Hells Angels chapter 1955–62, allegedly drove to Hollywood and purchased Marvin's legendary blue-and-yellow, horizontal block-striped sweater; he wore it through his entire term of office until it eventually fell to pieces.

Left: Reversible green and red satin Korean souvenir tour jacket with tiger head embroidery, 1950s, Korea. Cream wool three button vest, 1950s, England. Alloy army dog-tags, USA. Khaki webbing army belt, 1940s, England. Chrome key chain. Blue denim work jeans, 1950s, USA.

Above left: Black leather cross zip cut-off biker jacket, 1970s, England. Red and white striped cotton T-shirt. Black cotton turtle neck T-shirt. Pigskin leather flying goggles, 1950s. Metal key on a leather thong. Blue denim jeans, Levi's 501. Tan leather belt with German army brass buckle inscribed Einigkeit, Recht, Freiheit, (Unity, Justice, Freedom), 1950s, Germany.

Above right: Rust cotton denim work jacket, 1940s, USA. Grey cotton T-shirt. Red and white cotton bandana. Brown leather flying goggles, 1940s, England. Blue denim Ikeda dungarees, 1950s, USA. Tan leather belt.

Right: 1950s style American Highway Patrol cap, similar to the one worn by Marlon Brando in *The Wild One*.

Left: Fig 1. Brown suede fringed Western jacket, 1960s, USA. Yellow and black check shirt with V collar insert, early 1960s, England. Brown leather army belt. Blue denim jeans. Black leather work boots.

Fig 2. Royal blue and white striped wool cardigan, early 1960s, England. Yellow chiffon scarf. Black leather gloves. Bronze and black denim jeans, early 1960s, England. Brown burnished leather belt with brass horseshoe buckle. Black kitten heel pointed boots, 1960s, England.

Right: Fig 1. Brown sheepskin flying jacket, 1940s, England. Rust wools sweater with cream brick pattern yolk, 1950s, England. Grey denim jeans, 1960s, England. Enfield Villiers points cover and chains, 1960s, England. Black leather biker boots.

Fig 2. Navy wool donkey jacket, 1960s, England. Blue and grey check shirt, Measurmade, 1960s, England. Black leather belts and chains. Powder blue denim jeans, Citizen Shapes by Milletts, 1960s, England. Black leather work boots, 1960s, England.

Left: Fig 1. Blue denim jacket with fur trim, Levi's. Green brushed Orlon cardigan, 1960s, USA. Tan, cream and brown check polyester cowboy shirt, 1960s, USA. Bronze denim jeans, early 1960s, England. Brown PVC boots with fake curly lamb trim, early 1960s, England.

Fig 2. Blue denim jacket, Levi's. Brown and cream mohair, shawl collared sweater, early 1960s, England. Peach chiffon scarf. Silver locket on chain. Ricky Nelson portrait on a boxing shield plaque. Brown shot with black denim jeans, early 1960s, England. Black PVC boots, 1960s, England.

Fig 3. Blue denim jacket, Wrangler. Brown and tan fake fur leopard print waistcoat, 1970s, England. Fur neck scarf. Metal shell case on a chain. Black leather belt with metal spikes and rings. Black denim jeans. Black leather biker boots, early 1960s, England. Fox fur tail.

Right: Fairground rebels, Zürich, 1960, ©Karlheinz Weinberger.

Knights of the Road

After the Second World War, English motorbikes became very popular with the working class as an economical form of transport. Bikes such as Triumph, BSA and Royal Enfield, although basic, were well made, quite efficient and, with the aid of a handbook and a few basic tools, could easily be repaired by their owners. Many fathers would teach their sons the art of motorcycle maintenance in their own back yards or sculleries, fitting all types of accessories that would give more speed or greater efficiency. At weekends they would go off to a speedway or grass-track meet, and once a year the real enthusiasts headed off to the Isle of Man, to watch their heroes tear around the country lanes in the world-famous TT Races. And so by the early 1950s, a great tradition had begun, progressively handed down from father to son, and as teenagers became regular earners, all over England new and second-hand motorbikes were kick-started into life by their proud 16-year-old owners. With the newfound freedom that having a bike allowed, friends soon started their own clubs and gangs, spending their spare time working on their machines and going on runs together.

New types of protective wear were developed for this younger market such as oilskins and PVC overalls, but these, although waterproof, were cold and bulky, not to mention ugly. They may have been okay for fishing, but a fellow could hardly chat up a bird wearing one. Surplus stores would prove to be a good source of quality, ex-Army leather jerkins, RAF Irving-style sheepskin flying jackets and trousers, and these became a firm favourite with the young bikers being warm and also quite stylish. Occasionally American leather flying jackets appeared in British surplus stores, and enthusiasts eagerly snapped them up.

As the market for motorbikes became younger, the demand for British leather jackets, trousers and boots also grew. British manufacturers like Aviakit responded to the demand, and leather jackets became available in two distinct styles. The first was based on the American Perfecto jacket that had been introduced in 1935, so-called because it was 'perfect' for bikers, although it was mainly worn by state troopers and highway patrolmen. The jacket had a cross zip which gave more protection to the chest, four deep, zipped pockets, a pleated back for ease of movement, a sturdy belt at the waist, and a deep collar to which a fur collar could be attached. Marlon Brando would be seen in a Perfecto in *The Wild One*. The British version of this style was made from a narrower gauge hide, had fewer pockets, no fur collar and less detailing, but with its distinct red satin lining it was in some ways more stylish and certainly less cumbersome.

Above: Camel chunky knit shawl collar cardigan with blue, grey and black biker motifs, Mary Maxim, 1960s, England. White cotton T-shirt. Black leather biker goggles, Baruffaldi, 1960s, Italy. Black leather weightlifter's belt. Blue denim jeans, 1960s, England. Black leather cowboy boots with steer skull detail, Judy Rothchild for R Soles.

Left: Cream, red and black chunky knit cardigan with Indian totem pole motif, Mary Maxim, 1960s, England. Black cotton T-shirt. Red and white cotton bandana. Metal bullets on a chain. Black leather belt with horse brasses. Black denim jeans.

Above: Yellow suedette jacket with fake leopard print shawl collar, early 1960s, England. Cream wool cable knit sweater with shawl collar, 1960s, England. Chrome neck chain. Black leather belt with brass Elvis buckle. Black nylon ski-pants.

Right: Fig 1. Leopard print sweater, Orlon, 1960s, England. White chiffon scarf. Brown felt circle skirt with black flecks, early 1960s, England. Black patent belt. White leather side lace pointed stiletto shoes, Manuella, early 1960s, Italy.

Fig 2. Black PVC cross zip biker jacket with white details, Pride & Clarke, London, 1960s. Black and grey block striped cotton top, Beat Beat, 1980s, England. Khaki denim jeans, Levi's. Black leather biker boots, Lewis Leather Mike Hailwood TT, 1960s, England.

The other style of jacket had also been influenced by an American model, and had a straight zip, two slanted-zip breast pockets, zips on the cuffs, and side adjusters on the waistband. Both designs were popular but the cross zip was more expensive. For a little extra money, decorative fringing was also available, and each model came in PVC for those who could not afford the real thing. By the mid 1950s, most young kids who owned bikes were also wearing one of the new-style black leather jackets.

Noisy local gangs became notorious for upsetting quiet neighbourhoods, and illegal night-time street racing gave rise to many a ruck with opposing gangs. These new knights of the road revelled in their notoriety, and as word spread of their daring escapades so their numbers increased. Speed to these kids was the greatest thrill: to achieve 100 miles per hour on the open road was considered the ultimate goal, and because of this obsession they were nicknamed 'ton-up kids'.

Police officers all over Britain were instructed to put an end to what was seen as a growing menace by this new generation of thrill-seeking youths on the over-crowded roads. Individuals were singled out because of the way they looked or because they owned a motorbike and blamed for endless petty crimes. They got labelled as 'hoods', 'thugs', 'leather boys' and 'coffee-bar cowboys', and through the ever-hungry press they became the scourge of the nation. Some gangs were even infiltrated by police snatch squads, such was the importance of the threat they posed to everyday life.

By the late 1950s and early 1960s, the pride that had been previously shown in the boys' bikes was now being equalled by their dramatic appearance. Leather jackets labelled Bronx, Comet, Highway Patrol, Highwayman, Lightning, Thunderbolt and Whirlwind came with a variety of linings such as check flannel, fleece, fake fur and quilted red satin.

Jackets also began to be decorated with individual trophies, such as enamel and tin badges of bike logos, gangs, rallies, petrol and oil products, and embroidered patches bearing similar logos were lovingly sewn onto jackets. On the back of a jacket, some would hand paint heraldic-style symbols such as a death's head, a tiger's head, a skull and crossbones, a German eagle, cat's eyes, a pair of crossed pistons, a gang or club name, its motto and the owner's name, or the logo of the bike, in large white letters painted right across the back of the jacket. Chrome studs, nail heads and draped chains were also used to highlight names and logos.

A heavily studded leather belt was an essential, and white silk or satin opera scarves like those donned by Second World War fighter pilots were worn not only to protect the face from the elements but also to disguise the wearer's identity from the police.

Left: Black leather cross zip fringed biker jacket with Triumph patches, 1960s, England. Cream silk opera scarf, 1940s, England. Grey oiled wool seaman's sweater, 1950s, England. Black Lewis Leathers biker trousers, 1960s, England. Black leather belt with Triumph petrol tank emblem, 1960s, England. A pair of black leather and chrome Halcyon Mark 9 racing goggles, 1960s, England. Black leather biker boots, Lewis Leather Mike Hailwood TT, 1960s, England. White oiled wool seaman's socks.

Above: Rita Tushingham and Colin Campbell, *The Leather Boys*, dir Sidney J Furie, 1964.

Right: Black leather belt with Triumph petrol tank emblem, 1960s, England.

Above: PVC 1960s style milkman's cap customised with studs and chains.

Right: Black vinyl studded straight zip biker jacket with white piping, Tyne-Tex, 1960s, England. Grey fleck wool sweater. Black leather belt with chrome lions head buckle. Grey and black striped denim jeans, early 1960s, England. Black leather biker boots, Frank Thomas, 1970s.

Slim-fitting Westcott or Jet American-style jeans in black or blue denim with green or white stitching were very popular, also leather trousers that would be tucked into high leather boots, and white seamen's socks worn with the cuff showing over the top of the boots. Some bikers also wore rubber wellington boots, particularly in wet weather. Leather gauntlets were worn to protect hands from the weather, scuffs and falls. At that time, the law did not require crash helmets to be worn, but many kids sported the popular pudding-basin style helmets and ex-RAF flying goggles or Stadium Mark 1 goggles as worn by their speedway heroes. Underneath jackets, check work shirts in black and red, blue and red or black and green were worn unbuttoned at the neck with the collars turned up, under roll-neck or crew-neck oiled wool seamen's sweaters. Chunky, zip-front Mary Maxim Cowichan-themed cardigans were extremely popular and came in a wide range of graphic designs that featured hobbies and sports, such as angling, speedway, hunting and cricket, and even Indian totem poles.

This was the golden age of biking with thousands of kids being attracted to new clubs and gangs every year. In 1962, Father Bill Shergold, a motorcycling enthusiast, formed the 59 Club. Shergold, also known as the 'ton-up vicar', wanted to clean up the biker's bad image and give it respectability. The club was a huge success and by the mid 1960s its membership was over 7,000.

In 1964 a classic British biker movie, *The Leather Boys*, directed by Sidney J Furie, was released. The film, which is probably the best British biker film ever made, features all the great styles of the time. It has a realistic docudrama feel to it and was also quite controversial because of its homosexual content.

As the decade progressed, the whole look became more aggressive and military influenced. American outlaw biker gangs took to wearing denim cut-offs over their leathers. Known as 'colours', these jackets would generally have a rocker (or patch) on the back containing the name of the club, and this is where the nickname 'Rocker' came from.

British kids, like their American cousins, began wearing the SS regalia of Nazi Germany, trophies brought back from the Second World War by their fathers. This emotive imagery deliberately antagonised the older generation and the police, and enhanced their bad-boy reputation. Colours were adorned with Nazi Iron Crosses, swastikas, coded patches and club regalia. One patch the Hells Angels are particularly proud of is the '1%'. This dates back to 1960, when the AMA declared that 99 per cent of all American bikers were good people who just enjoyed the sport, but the remaining one per cent was comprised of antisocial barbarians living outside the law.

Steel toecap work boots, cowboy boots and pointed winkle-picker boots added to the look. Jeans with deep turn-ups were now worn over the top of the boots. Brando had first made highway patrol caps popular in *The Wild One*, and now English bikers started to wear black PVC-peaked caps that were traditionally worn by train drivers and milkmen. These prized trophies were adorned with chains, studs and badges and worn with great pride, as were the black-and-white-fringed cowboy hats with 'Kiss Me Quick' written across the front, found at fairgrounds and seaside resorts. Seasides had always been a natural draw for young people, and between 1964 and 1966 British promenades and beaches saw bloody battles between rival Mod and Rocker gangs take place.

Fairground Kids

I grew up in the country and during the late 1950s a highlight of the school holidays would be cycling with my mates to the annual funfair, which was a huge draw at a neighbouring village. This was a really big deal for an 11-year-old, and for some of us the funfair became a place of important rites of passage. It was also here amid the flashing neon lights, candyfloss and bubblegum, that I first became exposed to the exotic world of teenage Rockers, and infatuated by their tough-looking outfits.

The thing I most remember about these funfair visits was being truly terrified, intimidated by and yet in awe of the leather clad, greasy-quiffed Rocker kids that worked on the rides. Like car mechanics, their hands, faces and clothes were engrained with black swarf, oil and graphite from the rides. But to me they looked just like James Dean, Billy Fury and Gene Vincent, in their black leather biker jackets, and navy donkey jackets, always styled with the collar turned up. They also wore T-shirts, brand new to this country, and drainpipe jeans, battered winkle-pickers shoes, cowboy boots or steel toecap work boots.

And then there were those scary Rocker girls with their deathly make-up, huge bouffant hair-dos, pony tails, heavy kohl eyeliner, mascara and sloppy mohair sweaters, worn with cropped jeans or ski-pants and pointed pixie boots, who would hang around the most dangerous rides looking ultra cool, listening to 'Runaway' by Del Shannon or 'He's a Rebel' by the Crystals, 'Telstar' by the Tornados and 'Shakin' all Over' by Johnny Kidd & The Pirates being played really loudly.

But of course they were actually there to watch the boys perform their nightly ritual on the dodgems or bumper cars. This ride was the boys' main stage, a place where they could show off their seemingly effortless balletic skills by hopping from one car to another, without ever touching the electrified metal floor.

Then, balancing precariously on the back bumper, they would hang off the conducting poles like crazed banshees, and you can bet your life if a girl happened to be driving, one of the boys would grab the wheel and cause a collision, even though warning signs clearly stated 'No Bumping'. But the wildest rides were always the Waltzers. Here even the toughest looking Rocker girls would scream out loud as the boys rode the undulating platform and spun the cars around for a more intense ride. So cool! Although I was never a Rocker myself, the fast bikes and all the gear seduced several of my mates, so I always had the greatest respect for them.

In 2002 the London Photographers' Gallery mounted an amazing photographic exhibition of Rocker boys and girls, shot in the mid to late 1950s by a little-known gay Swiss magazine photographer named Karlheinz Weinberger. Suddenly I was swept back in time, surrounded by pictures of girls who looked just like the ones I had seen around the fairgrounds as a kid, with their big hair, shaggy mohair sweaters and tight jeans, and wonderful denim jackets, which were individually customised with Grolsch beer bottle pull tops replacing the buttons like trophies. Fantastic, how original – I don't think that detail was ever seen in England.

The boys, too, had all the trappings of American Rockers in their denim cut-off jackets, jeans and cowboy boots, but here again they had added their own over-sized talisman-like belt buckles, each one individually crafted from horse shoes, fur pelts, nuts, bolts and nail heads, and heavy metal plaques adorned with painted images of James Dean and Cliff Richard. These kids developed a raw tribal look that was as extreme as anything I have ever seen before, and it really reminded me of the unique crafted T-shirts Malcolm McLaren and Vivienne Westwood were later creating at their Kings Road shop Let it Rock in 1971.

Left: Blue denim 1960s style cut-off jacket with biker badges and patches, Wrangler.

Right: Fig 1. Black wool dress, 1960s, England. Silver neck chain. Black leather belt. Silver key chain. White PVC boots, 1960s, England.

Fig 2. Pale blue mohair sweater, 1960s, England. Chiffon leopard print neck scarf. Heavy chain worn as a necklace. Ice blue denim jeans, 1960s, England. White PVC majorette boots, 1960s, USA. Heavy ankle chain.

Fig 3. Blue denim 1960s style cut-off jacket with studs and biker patches, Wrangler. Black leather biker jacket, 1960s, England. Blue denim jeans, Levi's 501.

Fig 4. Blue denim 1960s style cut-off jacket with biker badges and patches, Wrangler. Blue denim jeans, Wrangler. Black leather biker boots, Lewis Leathers, 1960s, England.

Fig 5. Black vinyl studded straight zip biker jacket with white piping, Tyne-Tex, 1960s, England. Grey fleck wool sweater. Black leather belt with chrome lions head buckle. Grey and black striped denim jeans, early 1960s, England. Black leather biker boots, Frank Thomas, 1970s.

Left: Fig 1. Black leather cross zip biker jacket with red stripe and stud details, 1960s, England. White silk opera scarf with black fringe, 1950s, England. Black cotton T-shirt. Black leather studded belt. Black leather and metal stud wristbands. Black denim jeans. Black rubber wellington boots.

Left and right: Fig 2. Black rubberised cotton top with snakeskin print, 1960s, England. Cockerel's claw on a thong. Black patent belt. A pair of ivory winged sunglasses, early 1960s, England. Green taffeta circle skirt with black and cream spiral decoration, early 1960s, England. White leather pointed stiletto shoes, Mondaine, early 1960s, Italy.

Left and right: Black leather cross zip biker jacket with hand painted eagle and words Hen Angel daubed across the back, Blatt of Chicago, 1950s. This jacket was purchased by my wife Izabel from Let It Rock in the early 1970s.

Left: Fig 1. Black leather cut-off biker jacket with patches and Nazi regalia, 1960s, German. Black and white wool block stripe sweater. Metal chain and padlock. Black leather belt. Black denim jeans. Black leather biker boots, Lewis Leathers, 1960s, England.

Fig 2. Black leather straight zip biker jacket with fringing, SS patches and badges, 1960s, England. Black cotton roll-neck sweater. Black denim jeans. Black leather biker boots, Lewis Leathers, 1960s, England.

Above: Peter Fonda and Nancy Sinatra, *The Wild Angels*, dir Roger Corman, 1966.

Next page: Fig 1. Peacock blue wool poncho with black fringing, 1960s, England. Metal chain necklace. Black nylon ski-pants. Black leather boots with fur trim, 1960s, England.

Fig 2. Wine, grey and black striped cotton shirt, Prova, early 1960s, England. Mauve chiffon scarf. Black leather belt with cowboy buckle. Silver key chain. Maroon shot with black denim jeans with white stitching, early 1960s, England. Crimson suede pointed stiletto boots with black fringing, 1960s, England. Black leather dog collar.

Fig 3. Black leather cut-off biker jacket with patches and Nazi regalia, 1960s, German. Black and white wool block stripe sweater. Metal chain and padlock. Black leather belt. Black denim jeans. Black leather biker boots, Lewis Leathers, 1960s, England.

Fig 4. Black leather straight zip biker jacket with fringing, SS patches and badges, 1960s, England. Black cotton roll-neck sweater. Black leather studded wristbands. M1942 replica fiberglass German army helmet. Black denim jeans. Black leather biker boots, Lewis Leathers, 1960s, England.

Fig 5. Fake fur leopard print top, Robbie Bee, 1960s, Chicago. Black wool scarf, Black nylon ski-pants. Red vinyl pointed stiletto boots, 1960s, England.

Fig 6. Pale yellow cotton duster coat, 1960s, England. Grey sweater with pale grey turtle neck insert, Courtelle, 1960s, England. Silver locket and chain kindly loaned by Laura Nash. Black leather belts. Multi-link key chains. Black nylon ski-pants. Black PVC boots, 1960s, England.

5

TO DO IS TO BE

BEATS & BEATNIKS

EARLY 1950s – EARLY 1960s

"What is it like to be really cool? Not the heroin-induced coolness of the junkie nor the rather staged cooldom of the jazz fiend, but the philosophical, though unexpressed, coolness of the thousands of cats and chicks across the land to whom being cool is a virtue absolutely mountainous in dimension. Coolness is all. The cats regard something not cool as other people regard double pneumonia."

Chandler Brossard, *Dude* magazine, 1958.

As the dark days of the Second World War finally came to a close, individuals and small groups of free-thinking young people on both sides of the Atlantic started to experience a great sense of release, and two new cultural movements began to simultaneously emerge.

The originators of the American movement were referred to as 'Beats' and 'Hipsters'. The term 'Beat' had been first coined by author Jack Kerouac in the late 1940s, and is a mix of 'beat', as in 'dead beat' – exhausted and trampled down by conventional life and its emptiness – and 'beatitude' – blissful saintliness. 'Hipster' is a black slang term, meaning one who is hip, a hep cat. In 1960, the novelist Herbert Gold wrote an essay for *Playboy* magazine where he described a Hipster as *'a man who fled emotion through the use of narcotics, keeping cool, floating in his high'*. The original American Beats and their followers may have been predominantly white, but they revered many aspects of black culture, most notably the music and laid-back attitude to drugs.

In Britain and Europe, founder members of the movement were known as 'Bohemians': socially unconventional persons, especially artists and writers, of free and easy habits, manners, and sometimes morals, or 'Existentialists', who emphasised the existence of the individual person as a free and responsible agent, determining his or her own development. Bohemians and Existentialists took a great deal of inspiration from the American model, in particular the music they listened too, like free-form jazz, blues and folk, which had undoubtedly had African-American roots, although Paris had been a melting pot of American, African, Latin and Eastern music styles since the 1920s.

Compared to that of people in Europe, the average American's lifestyle had been little affected by the Second World War, and in some ways the nation thrived; farmers had been asked to produce even more food during the war to aid the Allied powers, with the promise of higher returns, and many American manufacturing companies profited as a direct result of the conflict. The Beats despised this blatant profiteering from other people's loss, sharing a great affinity with their downtrodden European equivalents, who had suffered first-hand the horrors and brutal reality of war. Although they were generally poor anyway, some Beats took to wearing old clothes as a protest against the sale of clothing, arms, food and raw materials overseas, having been exposed to this feeling of resentment over the War period by returning US troops and fleeing artists.

As citizens of an affluent nation who deplored all things that were old fashioned or even slightly worn, many Americans still discarded complete wardrobes full of perfectly good clothes just because they had become out-dated. Recycling was certainly not considered a priority to a country that had so many natural resources and, as a result, huge amounts of unwanted clothes either ended up in thrift shops to be bought by poorer people, or were simply burnt.

But one person's trash is another's treasure and, as a consequence, the attire that would be taken up by the European Beat movement came about as a direct result of America's plan to halt the spread of communism in Europe.

Various aid programmes were set up after the Second World War to help people who had been directly involved in the conflict, but by 1947 the American government was convinced that most of Europe was so poor it was about to turn communist. In order to combat this, they devised the Marshall Plan, a scheme to get aid and money into Europe to help countries rebuild after the War, and prevent the spread of communism through a return to prosperity.

Previous page: Marina Berti, *Deported*,
dir Robert Siodmak, 1950.

Above: *The Subterraneans*,
dir Ranald MacDougall, 1960.

Right: Fig 1. Tan leather jacket, 1950s, USA.
Grey shadow check shirt, Campus, USA. White
cotton T-shirt. Brown leather army belt. Khaki
army chinos, 1950s, USA. Black leather boots.

Fig 2. Pale blue cotton sweatshirt, 1950s,
USA. Brown trousers, Dickies 874, USA.
Tan leather, PF Flyers, USA.

Left: Fig 1. Black cowhide jacket, Californian, 1950s, USA. Black cotton T-shirt with Harvard University print. Khaki chinos, 1950s, USA. Black leather army boots, 1950s, England.

Fig 2. Green yellow and red striped cotton tunic dress, Kitty Copeland, 1950s, France. Black cotton roll-neck sweater. Ceramic lozenge on a leather thong. Black nylon ski-pants. Brown PVC fur trim ankle boots, 1950s, England.

Fig 3. Brown leather jacket, 1950s, USA. Red and grey check work shirt, 1950s, USA. White T-shirt. Brown cotton trousers, Dickies 874, USA. Cream plimsolls, 1950s, England. Brown leather belt.

Right: Burnt orange and black velvet smock top, Phil Rose of California, 1960s, USA. Black wool sweater. Brass and copper African talisman on a leather thong.

Above: Juliette Gréco at the entrance to Le Tabou, Paris, mid 1950s.

Right: Fig 1. Black cotton warehouse jacket, John Peck Leisurewear, 1950s, England. Rust and black block stripe cotton T-shirt, Beat Beat, 1980s, England. Metal discs on a leather thong. Grey flannel trousers, mid 1950s, England. Black and cream baseball boots, Empire Made, 1950s.

Fig 2. Deep red rayon shirt with striped insert and ribbing, Milwaukee Knit Products, 1950s, USA. Khaki chinos, 1950s, USA. Cream and black striped ticking espadrilles, Pare-Gabia, 1950s, France.

From 1948, the American government shipped vast quantities of grain, tinned foods, medicine, building materials and civilian and ex-military used clothes as aid to those European countries that had been affected by enemy occupation. France alone had tens of thousands of garments dumped on its doorstep. Before long, all kinds of American used clothing was being sold cheaply in Parisian street markets. Practical, utility-style clothes, such as second-hand American work wear, high-quality army and naval sweaters, pea coats, reefer jackets, trousers and boots, would be a welcome addition to the European Beats' everyday clothes. Another very popular winter coat in France at this time was called the Canadienne. Made from sheepskin, these especially warm coats had originally been imported from Canada during the First World War for soldiers in the trenches.

This donation was very timely, as money had become a scarce commodity, and in any case very little manufacture of new garments had taken place in the country in the preceding six years, forcing most people to wear older styles of clothes that they had bought before the War. Throughout the late 1940s and 1950s, American waste was the main source of used clothing, and the European Beat movement made good use of this endless supply.

People in Britain had also welcomed American aid and care packages, as rationing was not relaxed until the late 1940s. But as all classes still frowned upon the wearing of second-hand clothes, most normal people simply carried on with the 'make do and mend' policy recommended by the government during the War.

But to the new, free-thinking Beat movement all these government policies and class stigmas were irrelevant. Beats were dismissive of all frivolous fashion and of clothing in general, unless it was functional and understated, and in England as in America, the act of wearing used clothing as an anti-capitalist statement would become an important part of their ideology.

However, there was at least one item of practical clothing that ticked all the boxes when it came down to form and function, and that was the duffle coat (also referred to as the 'Monty coat' after the British war-hero General Montgomery, who favoured the style; in America they are known as a duffer coat). The duffle coat had been designed originally for Belgian fisherman before being adopted by the Royal Navy, as these heavy wool coats were warm, hard-wearing and simple in design. They came in basic navy, black or camel, had durable toggle buttons that could be easily undone by cold hands, and had a sensible hood. The duffle coat continued to be popular with all esoteric types in the UK right through to the mid 1960s.

Right: Fig 1. Black cheese cloth top. Metal Ban the Bomb pendant on leather thong. Blue wool dirndl skirt, John Travers, early 1960s, London.

Fig 2. Burnt orange and black velvet smock top, Phil Rose of California, 1960s, USA. Black wool sweater. Brass and copper African talisman on a leather thong. Black nylon ski-pants.

Fig 3. Black cotton warehouse jacket, John Peck Leisurewear, 1950s, England. Rust and black block stripe cotton T-shirt, Beat Beat, London. Metal discs on a leather thong. Grey flannel trousers, 1950s, England. Black and cream baseball boots, Empire Made, 1950s.

Howl and Other Poems, Allen Ginsberg, 1956, Courtesy of Laura Nash.

140

Convergence

Beats may not have given much time or thought to clothes or other material items, but right from the outset both the English and European movements had been energised by new forms of abstract expressionist art that were emerging from America.

Although this art was not well received by the general public at home, American abstract artists thrived during the 1940s and 1950s. This was mainly because of massive investment in all art genres by the government, who firmly believed that this particular expression of free Americanism had something new to say about freedom of thought, and would further promote their anti-communist stance. Many historians claim that abstract expressionist art was the first and only true American art, even though its inspiration had originally been drawn from European surrealism, dada and cubism. The message was loud and clear, and would be eagerly taken up by European artists who recognised that its creative spirit could be applied to any medium.

Although poles apart in many ways, the American and French movements were drawn together by like-minded philosophers and poets who sought refuge from the pressures of the urban environment and protested against its mechanisation and inhumanity. As a result, many originators of the Beat movement visited France after the War and absorbed its culture, from the cafés of Saint-Germain and hot jazz clubs in the Latin Quarter to the many artists' studios of Montmartre. The cross-fertilisation would continue right through the 1950s as travel became easier.

This like-mindedness was further underlined by those angst-ridden writers who hit the road laden with uppers and downers, artists who through abstract expressionism revealed unfinished canvases, musicians who played continuous free-form jazz with avant-garde sound effects; and filmmakers who created grainy, minimalist short films, with ad-libbing actors who prayed for failure. Devotees believed intensely in personal experience, freedom of speech, co-habitation, drug experimentation, sexual liberation, energy release and spontaneous activation. Improvised free-form poetry became a universal expression of the here and now, and was practised at any given opportunity.

The movement on the whole was very introverted and thrived on its alienation from regular society. To take this even further, Beats refined their own hip language or 'Beat speak', as it was known. 'Man', 'chicks', 'square', 'jerk', 'dig', 'cool', 'later', 'baby', 'too much', 'something else', 'groove', 'let's split', 'I'm bugged', 'pad', 'far out', were just some of the words and phrases in everyday use. The press, who had always been intrigued by the movement's indignation, desperately tried to commercialise the language by using it liberally in trite editorial spreads that in any way referred to fashion, music or the media.

Above: 1. Navy wool sailors cap.

2. Brown corduroy sailors cap.

3. Navy wool Basque beret.

Left: Fig 1. Black cotton tunic jacket, 1950s, England. Grey and black bird's eye cotton sweatshirt, Buckingham, 1950s, England. Khaki chinos, 1960s England. Black leather work boots.

Fig 2. Reversible white cotton windcheater with black ink splash print, 1950s, Ireland. Black roll-neck sweater. Black ski-pants. Black PVC pointed boots, 1960s, England.

Left: Fig 1. Black wool duffle jacket, Ashpool & Twiddy, 1960s, England. Red and white striped cotton turtle neck top, early 1960s, England. Blue denim jeans, early 1960s, England. Navy leather pumps, Moccasin, 1950s, England.

Fig 2. Navy wool duffle coat, Abbeygate British Tailored, 1960s. Red and blue brushed cotton work shirt, 1950s, England. Blue and white paisley cotton bandana. Blue denim jeans. Brown suede and leather crepe-soled desert boots.

Right: Fig 1. Black PVC raincoat, 1950s, England. Black and grey speckled wool seaman's sweater, 1960s, England. Grey wool trousers, 1950s, England. Black leather work boots.

Fig 2. Black PVC raincoat, Diamond Brand Maxron, 1960s, Scotland. Green plaid mohair tunic top, 1960s, England. Black roll-neck sweater. Black nylon ski-pants Black PVC boots, 1960s, England.

Left: Fig 1. Navy wool duffle coat, 1950s, England. Yellow cotton T-shirt with New York Herald Tribune print, similar to the one worn by Jean Seberg in *Breathless*, 1960. Green and black check cotton trousers, early 1960s, England. Black suede ballet pumps.

Fig 2. Camel car coat, St Michael, early 1960s, UK. Grey fine striped cotton roll-neck. Brown corduroy trousers, 1960s, England. Black leather work boots.

Right: Beat-style young man, London, 1953.

By the mid 1950s, intellectuals generally referred to the movement as the 'Beat Generation'; meaning young people with unconventional dress and behaviour, as an expression of social philosophy. However the mainstream press on both sides of the Atlantic were still unable to take the Beats' behaviour seriously and, by 1958, began using the nickname 'Beatnik' – a pun on the Russian Sputnik programme – as a flippant, derogatory term to describe anyone who even remotely looked as if they subscribed to the Beats' 'way out' lifestyle. Herbert Gold further referred to a Beatnik as an imitation Hipster, wearing the clothes and loitering at the door of the club, and a 'Hipnik' (a term not widely used) as a cross between a Hipster and a Beatnik.

One of the earliest depictions of a stereotypical Beat in film was in the 1953 movie *Roman Holiday* with a character played by Eddie Albert. The French starlet Brigitte Bardot had also typified the Beatnik girl look and attitude from the very start of her career in the early 1950s. Many young women saw Bardot as a role model and were inspired by her outspoken independence in a male dominated industry. In 1959, she became the subject of an essay called 'Brigitte Bardot and the Lolita Syndrome' written by the intellectual Simone de Beauvoir, where she describes Bardot as a *'locomotive of women's history'* and declares her as the first and most liberated woman of post-War France.

Left: Fig 1. Navy wool pea coat, C Louis Weber, 1960s, USA. Red green and blue striped wool college scarf, 1960s, Belfast graduate. Black and white striped cotton T-shirt. Brown cotton work trousers, Dickies 874, USA. Black leather shoes.

Fig 2. Black leather threequarter-length coat, 1960s, England. Black and white striped cotton top, 1960s, England. Black nylon ski-pants. Black suede pumps.

Fig 3. Khaki canvas army cape, 1960s. Black and white striped cotton T-shirt, Beat Beat, 1980s, London. Black nylon ski pants. Black canvas plimsolls.

Fig 4. Grey heavy wool overcoat, 1940s, England. Light grey and cream check cotton work shirt 1950s, England. Grey wool trousers, 1950s, England. Black leather boots.

The Trendex

Chandler Brossard made the following observations in *Dude* magazine in 1958, describing what he sees as a new attitude taken on by 'cool', free-thinking girls at the time. He refers to this typical character as the 'Trendex'.

'If she is going to a party that night she will take herself. No one will call for her. (Uncool). At the party, she will probably know everyone present, but she will under no condition exhibit anything but the most casual and glacial interest in them. The Trendex won't drink very much, probably only a little wine or beer. She won't say very much either, probably limiting herself to comments on the hi-fi, which will play incessantly. She may – or she may not – go to bed with one of the cats. If she declines an invitation (she may not even get one), she will do it with indifference but – and this is the coolness – if she accepts she will do so with the same 'who cares?' dispassion. She could conceivably have more than one cat that night, but if she does she will be rigid about not showing the slightest preference. She will go home early (staying excessively late is not cool simply because it is an excess) and she will go home alone, as she came.'

Right: Fig 1. Green and beige check tweed jacket, Saxon Hawk styled by Huntsman, 1960s, Savile Row, London. Red and black abstract print cotton top with black polo neck insert, 1960s, England. CND badge. Brown corduroy trousers, 1960s, England.

Fig 2. Brown corduroy jacket, Count Christie, 1960s, England. Brown and white fleck wool seaman's sweater, 1960s, England. Black wooden African carving on leather thong. Green tweed trousers, 1960s, England. Brown leather sandals, 1960s, England.

Fig 3. Black and white fake fur pony skin top, 1960s, USA. Black nylon ski-pants. Black canvas plimsolls.

Fig 4. Red cotton play suit, 1960s, USA. Black suede pumps.

Fig 5. Green and beige check work shirt, 1960s, England. Blue and white striped cotton top. Buff and white cotton paisley bandana. Khaki cavalry twill trousers, 1950s, England. Tan leather sandals, Grenson, 1960s, England.

Fig 6. Grey and white striped shirt, 1960s, USA. Wooded beads. Stone chinos, 1960s, USA. Stone cotton espadrilles, Baso-Arte, 1960s, Spain.

Fig 7. Orange linen shift dress with black fringing, 1960s, Spain. Black nylon catsuit.

Above: Red Door Gallery, Detroit, 1963, ©Leni Sinclair.

Right: Fig 1. Brown corduroy jacket, Count Christie, 1960s, England. Brown and white fleck wool seaman's sweater, 1960s, England. Black wooden African carving on leather thong. Green tweed trousers, 1960s, England. Brown leather sandals, 1960s, England.

Fig 2. Green and beige check tweed jacket, Saxon Hawk styled by Huntsman, 1960s, Savile Row, London. Red and black abstract print cotton top with black polo neck insert, 1960s, England. CND badge. Brown corduroy trousers, 1960s, England. Brown leather sandals, 1960s, England.

The Beatnik persona fit perfectly with the dingy surroundings that these creatures inhabited. Their favourite meeting places were dark cellars and underground clubs, such as Le Tabou in Paris. Here, they could express themselves freely through intellectual conversation, poetry and free-form dance. An observer at the time noted that on the dance floors of jazz clubs, the 'Beatnik Convulsion' was all the rage. Stripping aside material things allowed the mind and body to be free and liberated, creating a sense of aloofness and mystic sensibility that normal society abhorred. Day and night, the Left Bank cafés of Saint-Germain became the exclusive meeting places and haunts of the movement.

Philosophers, such as Jean-Paul Sartre, would hold court for hours at Café de Flore surrounded by eager disciples and bright young things, like Juliette Gréco and Brigitte Bardot. Café de Flore was also a meeting place for the Parisian rich and famous and, as the Beat movement grew, even the elite became attracted to its new realism. Each city in the world had its own bohemian hangouts and coffee bars similar to the ones in Paris – the North Beach area and City Lights bookstore in San Francisco, Greenwich Village and Café Bizarre in New York, and Heaven and Hell and The Macabre in London's Soho. Even my hometown of Leicester had a dive bar called The Pit, with its typically dingy candlelit alcoves inhabited by bearded, beret-wearing characters playing chess or philosophising with each other over black coffee and French cigarettes.

In 1957 the hit musical *Funny Face*, directed by Stanley Donen, was released. The storyline follows a cute, free-thinking Beatnik girl, played by Audrey Hepburn, who is discovered in a Greenwich Village bookshop by a high-fashion photographer, played by Fred Astaire, who persuades her to become a model. He takes her off to Paris, where she runs away and joins the Left Bank Beat scene. The film was a huge success and largely responsible for bringing the Beatnik style into the limelight. Before long, boutiques and mainstream shops, particularly in France, were selling the look in its entirety.

Girls got the latest short, elfin haircuts, like those seen on the 1950s film stars Audrey Hepburn, Leslie Caron and Jean Seberg. Also, ponytails, fringes and deathly white make-up, topped off with winged sunglasses, created the essential look. Loose-fitting, heavy knit sweaters and tops called 'Sloppy Joes', sometimes worn the wrong way around with the V at the back, over black leggings or ski-pants, formed the all-familiar silhouette. Large hooped earrings or even a single silver earring were all the rage. Both sexes took to wearing beads, silver medallions, crucifixes, small sculptures made from stone,

shell, bones, wood or other found objects on thongs or as brooches. Sculptural jewellery designs, inspired by those created by New Yorker Sam Kramer, were very popular.

The Party Is Over

By the end of the decade, Beatniks had become figures of fun, and illustrators and comic-strip artists grabbed every opportunity to put them down or send them up in the media. Typical caricatures saw tall, sickly-looking skinny boys wearing traditional Basque-style berets and either matelot striped tops or black polo-neck sweaters and white jeans. Others were depicted wearing check or plaid work shirts, neck scarves and ill-fitting trousers. All had Van Dyke or goatee beards, wore sandals of every type in all weathers, and heavy rimmed dark glasses, day or night. Some even had eye patches – an essential addition for an extra-cool intellectual image. Actually, the above description could apply to any number of genuine Beats and Beatniks on the scene in London, Paris or New York. By this time, the look had also been taken up by college students in England, and a new breed of teenager called 'Trads' (kids who were into the trad jazz, folk and skiffle scene) had emerged.

Left: Fig 1. Green and beige check work shirt, 1960s, England. Blue and white striped cotton top. Buff and white cotton paisley bandana. Khaki cavalry twill trousers, 1950s, England. Tan leather sandals, Grenson, 1960s, England.

Fig 2. Grey and white striped shirt, 1960s, USA. Wooded beads. Stone chinos, 1960s, USA. Stone cotton espadrilles, Baso-Arte, 1960s, Spain.

Above: Oliver Reed, *The Party's Over*,
dir Guy Hamilton, 1965.

Right: Cream silk blouse with hand painted
town square street scene and music notes,
Emilio Pucci, 1960s, Florence, Italy.
Black nylon ski-pants.

Above: Back cotton top. White cotton skirt with abstract black brushes and green and yellow paint splashes print.

Right: Fig 1. Blue cotton top with yellow vase print, 1960s, England. Black wool roll-neck sweater. Black nylon ski-pants.

Fig 2. Navy cotton artist's smock, England. Blue and white striped cotton top. Black nylon ski-pants.

In 1959, the recently formed Campaign for Nuclear Disarmament (CND) organised a huge protest rally and march from the centre of London to the Aldermaston Atomic Weapons Establishment, which attracted masses of left-wing intellectuals, liberal politicians, radical free thinkers and Beatniks. There is a fascinating documentary about the march, shot at the time by radical filmmaker Lindsay Anderson, called *The March to Aldermaston*, which records the varied Beatnik styles of the time.

The years that followed saw the release of several Beat-and Beatnik-influenced films: the inspired *Pull My Daisy*, 1959, by director Robert Frank, starring Allen Ginsberg and narrated by Jack Kerouac; pure exploitation with *Beat Girl*, 1960, and *The Subterraneans*, 1960; and a comedy called *The Rebel*, 1961. Finally, the aptly titled *The Party's Over*, 1965, directed by Guy Hamilton and starring the wonderfully moody Oliver Reed, which centres on a group of hedonist Chelsea Beatniks called the Pack, took three years to get past the censor because of its overlying message and scenes of 'bad taste'. By way of protest both the director and producer asked for their names to be removed from the credits. The following introductory voiceover is read by Oliver Reed and appears before the titles:

> 'This film is the story of some young people who chose to become – well, for want of a better word – "Beatniks". It's not an attack on Beatniks; the film has been made to show the loneliness, and the unhappiness, and the essential tragedy that can come from a life lived without love for anyone or anything. Living only for kicks is not enough.'

Although the music, writing, poetry, art and filmmaking produced by the Beat movement left a lasting cultural impression on the generations that followed, shortly after the time of conception each of the above eventually fell victim to cynicism and fashion.

> 'The world is hot and getting hotter but we'll play it cool man, way out and way cool.'

Chandler Brossard, *Dude* magazine, 1958.

6

THE 'IN' CROWD

MODERNISTS & MODS

MID 1950s – MID 1960s

"College-boy smooth crop hair with burned in parting, neat white Italian rounded-collared shirt, short Roman jacket very tailored (two little vents, three buttons), no turn-up narrow trousers with 17-inch bottoms absolute maximum, pointed toe shoes and a white mac lying folded by his side." Of Dean Swift.

Absolute Beginners, Colin MacInnes, 1958.

Legend has it that while holidaying in Italy in 1956, Cecil Gee, London tailor to the stars, was alerted to the latest emerging 'Italian look' or 'Roman style' being developed by leading tailors, such as Brioni in Rome. Gee was so inspired by this new shape he decided to produce his own version for the English market, considering it to be the next big thing in modern menswear.

Gee's streamlined Italian look consisted of a short, sharp, slim silhouette and a new use of lightweight fabrics in an assortment of rich but subtle colours and patterns. Bum-freezer jackets, super-slim trousers and pointed toe shoes were the order of the day and in no time small groups of young men called 'Modernists' adopted this new streamlined style of dressing.

Modernists are often hailed as the originators of the birth of cool. Eager to disassociate themselves from the garishly dressed Teddy Boys – who by this time were being constantly condemned by the press for their reputation for violence and bad behaviour – these guys must have looked like aliens in their sharp suits and shorty macs, drifting in and out of the new Italian-style espresso bars and bohemian jazz cellars of Soho, where they listened to the latest modern jazz imports and black R&B sounds from America.

In the early 60s I remember begging my mum to buy me a pair of Denson fine point winkle-picker shoes that I had spotted in a Melton Mowbray shoe shop. They were a mustard toned light tan leather with black shadows around the minimalist broguing on the toe, and I loved them. I wore them with tight bronze denim jeans and a dark brown needle cord boxy bum-freezer jacket with two-inch side vents, a white giraffe neck tab collar shirt, and thought I was the bee's knees.

In 1962, a British movie called *The Boys*, directed by Sidney J Furie, hit cinemas. The film, a social melodrama about the suspected murder of a night watchman by four teenage boys, readily illustrates the widespread discrimination directed at post-War youth by a conservative society. This point is further driven home by the adult witnesses, intimidated by the boys' outlandish appearance and dress codes, and antagonised by their threatening behaviour. Furie's close study of the boys – who all sport the latest Italian slim-line style – highlights their immaculate winkle-picker shoes, Slim Jim ties and three-point handkerchiefs. The film also emphasises the then-current trend for 'bold stripes' – traditionally associated with social outcasts since the eighteenth century – printed on their shirts, ties, suits and even a raincoat. Male narcissism is constantly referred to and observed through the use of such accessories as a cigarette holder, and a switchblade knife used not only for manicuring the nails but also inevitably as the murder weapon. Infamous East End gangsters the Kray Brothers were always immaculately turned out and regularly photographed wearing the 'Italian Look' during their illustrious career.

As the Modernist movement grew so styles developed and, in September 1962, the influential *Town* magazine ran a fashion editorial feature entitled 'Faces Without Shadows' about a small group of friends from north London. Mainly Jewish and very much products of a new affluent middle-class society, to them buying fashionable clothes was like a religion, and they were always on the lookout for new shapes and materials. Among the group was an outspoken 16-year-old youth called Marc Feld, who would later become pop star Marc Bolan. Marc and his peers were immaculately dressed in the article and all shared an obsession with style, while displaying a certain posing attitude that became *de rigueur* for many Mods. The attention to detail found in their tailor-made clothes and accessories and clever use of colours were soon to capture the imagination of the nation's youth, and this seminal magazine feature was to be the launch pad for a new form of purist Mods. It is most likely where the term 'Face', to describe top Mods, came from.

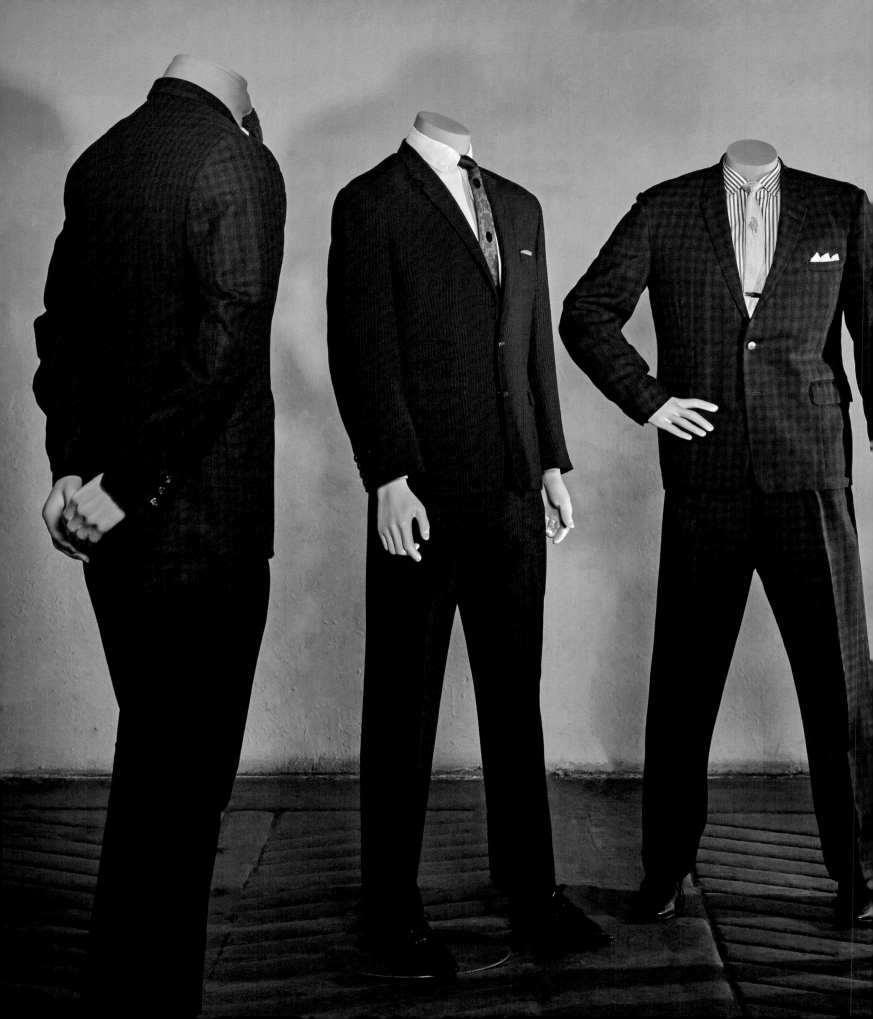

Previous page and below: Dudley Sutton, *The Boys*, dir Sidney J Furie, 1962.

Left: Fig 1. Black and gold check wool Italian style three button suit, Hardy Amies for Hepworths, late 1950s, England. Deep yellow cotton tab collar shirt, Altschiller & Friedman, 1960s, Brooklyn NY. Green and brown hand woven Slim Jim tie, early 1960s, England.

Fig 2. Brown and black striped two button wool Italian style suit, Paul Taylar, late 1950s, Hounslow, England. Pink cotton button-down shirt, Colebrooke, early 1960s, USA. Bronze and black paisley and polka dot silk tie, Lago di Como, late 1950s, Italy. Black leather with brown mock croc detail winkle-pickers, Denson, late 1960s, London.

Fig 3. Black and chestnut brown shadow check wool two button Italian style suit, Peter Pell, late 1950s, England. Brown and white striped cotton shirt, Double Two, late 1950s, England. Cream Slim Jim tie with bronze feather motif, Distinctive Ties, late 1950s, England. Gilt tie clip with black plastic detail, late 1950s, England. Black leather lace up winkle-picker shoes, late 1950s, England.

Fig 4. Navy blue slub silk two button suit, B. Ferszt & Son, 1959, Sackville St W1. Navy and white gingham tab collar shirt, Wemblex, 1960s, England. Grey, white and blue horizontal stripe Terylene Slim Jim tie, Meakers of Piccadilly, 1960s, London. Black mock snakeskin fine point winkle-pickers, Johnsons, 1980s, London. This suit was worn by Phil Collins in the video for 'You Can't Hurry Love', 1982.

Above: 1. Black fine point winkle-pickers, early 1960s, England.

2. Black leather and brown mock croc detail winkle-pickers, Denson, early 1960s, England.

3. Black leather 1960s style winkle-picker shoes with red saddle stitching, Shelleys, 1980s, London.

Right: Black and gold check wool Italian style three button suit, Hardy Amies for Hepworths, late 1950s, England. Deep yellow cotton tab collar shirt, Altschiller & Friedman, 1960s, Brooklyn NY. Green and brown hand woven Slim Jim tie, early 1960s, England.

Left: Fig 1. Stone cotton shortie mac with bamboo buttons, Plymouth, early 1960s Boston, England. Navy and white gingham tab collar shirt, Wemblex, 1960s, England. Grey, white and blue horizontal stripe Terylene Slim Jim tie, Meakers of Piccadilly, 1960s, London.

Fig 2. Gunmetal finish shortie mac, Kattex, late 1950s, England. Brown and white striped cotton shirt, Double Two, late 1950s, England. Cream Slim Jim tie with bronze feather motif, Distinctive Ties, late 1950s, England.

Fig 3. Bronze finish collarless shortie mac with Edwardian top pocket detail, Aquastorm, early 1960s, England. Pink cotton button-down shirt, Colebrooke, early 1960s, USA. Bronze and black paisley and polka dot silk tie, Lago di Como, late 1950s, Italy.

Below: White cotton shirt with faint red stripes, and rounded pin-through collar, Wemblex, early 1960s, England. Both Malcolm McLaren and I unearthed large amounts of these early 1960s deadstock shirts from a Portsmouth factory in the mid 1970s. Sold originally to revivalists, they were eventually crafted into Anarchy shirts by Vivienne Westwood for Seditionaries.

Left: Fig 1. Cream and tan slub silk two button bum freezer jacket, Jainsons West End, late 1950s, London. Peach cotton self-stripe rounded collar shirt, David Jonathan, late 1950s, England. Black cotton knitted tie, 1960s, England. Black leather early 1960s style waistcoat, England. Black wool slim-line slacks, 1960s, England. Black mock snakeskin fine point winkle-pickers, Johnsons, 1980s, London.

Fig 2. Olive and black check single button wool bum freezer jacket with two inch side vents, early 1960s, England. Light green angora sports shirt with darker green side panels, early 1960s, Italy. Light green three-point pocket handkerchief. Olive Trevira slim-line slacks, early 1960s, England. Black leather winkle-picker shoes with red saddle stitching, Shelleys, 1980s, London.

Right: Marc Feld (Bolan) and friends, Faces Without Shadows, *Town* magazine, 1963, ©Don McCullin.

Above: 1. Tan suede chisel top shoes, Denson, early 1960s, England.

2. Brown leather chisel toe shoes, Rapallo, late 1950s, Italy.

3. Tan suede almond toe side buckle shoes, Italian Style, late 1950s, England.

Right: Fig 1. Bronze sleeveless sheath dress with velvet bow detail, late 1950s, England. Brown plastic fake snakeskin stiletto shoes, Princess, England.

Fig 2. Gold twill late 1950s Italian style suit with bum freezer jacket, five-inch side vents, slim-line trousers with notch cuff detail, D&G Tailors, Ingrebourne, England. Cream cotton splay collar shirt, Van Heusen, late 1950s, England. Cream three-point pocket handkerchief. Bronze and black silk Slim Jim tie with diamond and chevron detail, late 1950s, England. Tan suede almond toe side buckle shoes with saddle stitch detail, late 1950s, England.

Above: Fig 1. Tan suede collarless skirt suit with black leather trim, Saks Fifth Avenue, early 1960s, USA. Tan and green abstract print silk neck scarf, early 1960s, England.

Fig 2. Camel and black houndstooth wool casual jacket, Michael's MAN Boutique, early 1960s, London. Beige knitted cotton sports shirt with red and brown vertical side stripes, Spindletex, early 1960s, England. Camel mohair tapered trousers, early 1960s, England.

Right: Fig 1. Peach mohair cowl neck sweater, Jaeger, early 1960s, England. Peach and black striped velour trousers, early 1960s, England. Blue leather chisel toe slingback shoes with snakeskin insets, Mario Costa, early 1960s, Italy.

Fig 2. Brown wool short sleeved top with cream band detail, Marshall Field & Co, early 1960s, Hong Kong. Burnt orange and black shadow check mohair skirt, early 1960s, England. Brown pearlised chisel toe shoes, Panda by Debrett, early 1960s, England.

Fig 3. Deep yellow knitted polyester short sleeved top, Cadillac, early 1960s, New York. Lettice cotton tapered slacks with cargo pocket, Arne, early 1960s, Sweden. Yellow suede mock croc embossed chisel toe shoes with black lace front, Aronde, early 1960s, England.

The Blossoming

Although Gee had started out as one of the main suppliers of the new Italian look in London from his shop in Charing Cross Road, by the early 1960s there were numerous specialist menswear shops in and around Soho. These stores sold everything from imported Italian driving shoes with a chamfered heel, and French knitwear, to American Ivy League casual wear and, of course, original Levi's 501 shrink-to-fit blue jeans, which at this time were very rare, but would soon become a staple in almost every Mod's wardrobe.

The 501 jeans were generally worn with either the cuff turned under to add to the tubular shape, or with a one-inch turn-up, and they always looked best when they were new, because they were really stiff with dressing and held their shape. They were rarely washed after the first long ritual soaking while worn in a hot bath, and more likely replaced with a new pair if they started to look tired.

Tailored leather and suede jackets and full-length or mid-calf coats in muted colours such as maroon, bottle green, grey blue, brown, camel or mustard for men became really popular; some guys even wore bright red or even pink long suede coats. Jackets became longer and more fitted, and trousers straight-cut or with a slight flare. Mohair was the fabric of choice, as it was for their soul-singing idols, and pretty soon every local tailor was making his individual version of the look. By 1963, a number of retail shops had opened in Carnaby Street, London, selling the new Mod style off the peg. These colourful French-style boutiques were the brainchild of John Stephen, a young Scotsman, who had seen the potential of this new vibrant youth movement that liked to spend money, and he was quick to supply the very latest styles to fashion-hungry Mods at reasonable prices. And with styles changing almost daily, kids flocked there, while the more discerning Mods tended to shop at John Michael, Sportique, Ravel, Austin's, Raoul and Austin Reed, where they would get a more exclusive look.

Of all the exclusive imported men's styles available at the time, one cannot underestimate the influence of the American Ivy League style on British Mods, and this is probably because of its association with those elitist classes who attended American universities such as Harvard and Yale. The style was most popular in American menswear circles during the late 1950s and first half of the 1960s, and the young President John F Kennedy would epitomise the look in his sack suits. Its conservative clean-cut silhouette was softer, subtle and quite fresh when compared with previous American men's fashions, talked about in Chapter One. The 'sack suit', as it was known, can be traced back to the Edwardian era and was a loose, unfitted casual style that had a natural shouldered single-breasted jacket with two or three buttons.

The top button would be folded back behind the lapel, and the bottom button was left undone. It generally had a single hook vent and no darts. Trousers had turn-ups but were flat fronted with no pleats, and usually worn with a pair of either wingtip brogues or slip-on penny loafers, so called because they had a strip of leather across the front of the shoe with a slit in it to securely hold a penny for emergency phone calls. These perennial classics, brand named 'Weejuns', were created by G H Bass in 1936, and became a staple for both boys and girls.

In 1939, *Look* magazine ran a fascinating article about students on the Princeton campus in New Jersey who all wore the Ivy League look. What is so interesting about the photos is that they could have easily been taken 20 years later. For the article features a group of young men wearing button-down collar shirts, foulard ties, soft shouldered two- and three-button Harris tweed or herringbone jackets all worn with the bottom buttons undone, flannel slacks, argyle socks and white buck shoes. Their biggest statement was that none wore hats, at a time when practically every other man on the street wore some kind of headwear. Incidentally, during his short term in office, President Kennedy was often accused of killing the hat trade by his refusal to wear one. When looking at films of the 1960s, perhaps the most influential American actor to British Mods was Steve McQueen, who wore his own variation of the Ivy League look so effortlessly in *Love with the Proper Stranger*, 1963, *The Cincinnati Kid*, 1965, *The Thomas Crown Affair*, 1968 and, best of all, *Bullitt*, 1968.

Mods of this period were true individualists, so styling yourself or putting together an outfit was a creative process. You would never follow a label or design brand for an entire look, because you needed to look different to everyone else and become the one who others were envious of, so new ideas were always sought after, with inspiration being drawn from many sources. Mods were heavily influenced by French culture, and likewise French Mods, or Minets, were fascinated with *'le style Anglais'* – English clothes and music. French Mods could often be seen hanging out at affluent English seaside towns, like Bournemouth and Brighton in the mid 1960s, soaking up the style while wearing immaculate French versions of the look teamed with authentic English and American attire. Super-fine Scandinavian and Swiss lightweight fabrics and light colours, coupled with classic English Edwardian details, were very popular for suits, and even department stores like C&A began stocking great European suits off the peg to meet the demand.

Casual looks became more and more popular. American style wash-and-wear materials were used extensively in the manufacture of jackets, such as madras checks and plaids, seersucker pale blue-and-white striped ice cream jackets. I remember getting my first pair of Lee Jeans in 1964, which were a similar cut to Levi's 501s but were a looser fit from the knee down, giving the impression they were slightly flared. Worn at half-mast they looked great over suede desert boots, Hush Puppies or bowling shoes. Italian style knitted shirts were another Mod essential, some of the best had thick offset racing stripes, but if you couldn't afford the real thing there were always Fred Perry polo shirts, which were favoured by scooter kids. British company John Smedley still make a luxury knitted shirt in a similar style to the Italian ones from the 1960s.

For a Mod to have as many as six suits, all tailor-made, in his wardrobe was not uncommon. Top Mods were even known to stand up on buses and trains so as not to crease their finely cut suits. Functional pockets were kept to a minimum to avoid ruining the line, leaving room only for a comb, money, club membership cards, some speed and chewing gum. Shirts, knitwear and accessories, such as ties, tie-pins, cufflinks, hankies, scarves, watchstraps and socks, were bought weekly. Tan pigskin leather driving gloves with an oval cut-out on top of the wrist and small cut-outs over the knuckles were very popular at one point. As many as four pairs of immaculate shoes would be packed neatly alongside other complete outfits, as well as an expensive bottle of aftershave and the essential can of hair lacquer, in bowling bags ready for a weekend of posing. Dry-cleaning bills were high and everything had to be pressed before use.

Left: Fig 1. Grey three button mohair suit with ticket pocket, two ten-inch side vents, Burton Tailoring, 1964-66, England. Grey silk pocket handkerchief. Grey wool knit shirt with contrast grey stripe detail, Tigi Wear, Italy. Black leather imitation whale hide chukka boots, with strap fastening mid 1960s, England.

Fig 2. Grey woven sleeveless wool shift dress with houndstooth trim, 1964-66, England. Black leather and black and white dogtooth fabric pointed slingback kitten heels shoes, Fine Footwear, mid 1960s, England.

Fig 3. Slate blue three button mohair suit with two ten-inch side vents, Burton Tailoring, 1964-66, England. Cornflower blue button-down Oxford cotton shirt with thick coral stripes, Peter Golding, mid 1960s, England. Coral pocket handkerchief. Oxblood Cordovan leather lace up brogues, mid 1960s, USA.

Left: Battersea Mods in suede and leather coats from Bedlows, Berwick Street, Margaret St, London, 1963.

Right: Fig 1. Sand mohair three button suit with ticket pocket and twelve-and-a-half-inch jacket centre vent, pocketless straight legs trousers with guards style sloping cuffs, Allsopp Brindle & Boyle, 1964-66 London. Camel Botany wool polo neck sweater. Cream silk pocket handkerchief. Suede almond toe shoes, Hush Puppies, mid 1960s, England.

Fig 2. Bottle green tailored mohair skirt suit jacket with a Peter Pan collar, concealed pockets and a fifteen-inch centre vent, 1964-66, England. Dark brown patent strap shoes, Devonshire Freedom, mid 1960s, England.

These immaculate characters were often accused of being gay, particularly by the Rockers who despised their effeminate appearance, and indeed many of the 'ace faces' who worked in the boutiques around Carnaby Street were homosexual. But it was these guys who fired their customers' insatiable desire for the latest looks, sounds and smells, and they were always guaranteed to have up-to-date news about what was happening on the scene.

Between 1962 and 1966, the look developed almost weekly, and as the movement grew so a hierarchy developed: from the top Mods, who were called 'faces', 'stylists', 'individualists' and 'tickets', and whom the press nicknamed 'peacocks' because they posed and bought new clothes all the time. The lower ranks were called 'numbers', referring to the numbers printed on their T-shirts, sevens and sixes, who wore 7/6d T-shirts from cheap shops like Woolworths, 'states' and 'toy towns' who tried to emulate the looks of their heroes, but in reality could often only afford an American surplus parka, T-shirt, jeans and the haircut. Bluebeat hats became very popular when this West Indian music hit the scene. These tall crown hats had a stingy brim and wide Petersham ribbon hat band, similar to men's trilby hats of the 1920s and early 1930s. Long before wearing a crash helmet became compulsory, scooter kids would often wear Bluebeat hats, navy French-style berets, pork pie hats or golf hats for protection against the weather.

By 15 I had left school and got a job on the farm. The Mod movement was in full swing and I worked all hours God sent to afford the latest gear. The style was incredibly seductive to a young country boy, and I became totally immersed in all the detail, hidden codes and subtlety that was essential to the look. It was all about being immaculate, individual and ahead of the pack. Kids would outdo each other by having more buttons on the cuffs of their jackets, deeper vents, or inverted pleats. I was always picking up on subtle details of other Mods' suits across a darkened dancefloor. I remember thinking I was incredibly chic when I ordered a grey herringbone suit with semi-circular pocket flaps from Hepworths in Leicester. It cost about £15, or three weeks' wages... I adored the entire scene, the music, the dances, the drugs... It was elitist and narcissistic but it was the first time kids from whatever background could display their creativity and sexual ambiguity through clothes without toeing the line.

Left: Mods, Putney, London 1964.

Above: 1. A pair of gilt and pearl cufflinks, with a secret compartment for stashing pep pills, England, mid 1960s.

2. Alloy sports car steering wheel cufflinks on knitted driving gloves with tan leather palms, England, 1964-66.

Right: Fig 1. Yellow cotton Harrington style jacket, navy wool scarf with paisley print, white denim jeans, Levi's.

Fig 2. Stone open weave four button jacket, John Stephen for His Clothes, Carnaby Street, London, 1965. Orange rayon scarf with paisley print, red silk pocket hankie, beige cotton jeans, Levi's.

Speed

Although Mod was predominantly a male-driven movement, this was the beginning of unisex, and it attracted a strong following of girls who also adopted the look. Simple stylish shift dresses, boyish trouser suits, jackets, shirts and super-androgynous short haircuts *à la* Jean Seberg in *Breathless*, 1960, were the order of the day. Mod girls tended to keep in the background or maybe dance together, particularly at clubs, when the boys always danced together.

Mods needed to be exclusive, elitist, energetic and immaculate at all times. For some purists, Mod became a total way of life with their obsession fuelled by 'pep pills' that, when taken in large amounts, contained enough speed to stay awake for a whole weekend of action. Amphetamine, Dexedrine, Drinamyl nicknamed French Blues, Purple Hearts, Black Bombers, dubes, leapers, speed, were relatively easy to obtain, as some came in the form of slimming pills, especially if you knew someone, who worked at a chemist, or even better at Boots, the manufacturers, as I did. That is, until the police understood what they were dealing with and made them illegal. The term 'blocked' meant being high on any of the above drugs. But of course with every up there is a down, and the terms 'come down' and 'the horrors' refer to the after effects of taking the above drugs, which could be truly horrible for a couple of days. But as Friday night rolled around, you were ready to do it all over again. No one ever drank alcohol then – that was for squares – but plenty of coffee, Coca Cola and French cigarettes were enough to keep you going in between highs.

Top Mods would often be seen carrying a brand new surf, soul, R&B or Motown import LP record around, or even a rolled copy of the *Financial Times* to match a shirt, or a furled umbrella, posing in coffee bars by day and doing the latest dances at the best all-nighters.

The weekly British TV show *Ready Steady Go!* (1963-6), fronted by Mod queen and trendsetter Cathy McGowan, had a huge influence on the movement. She even had her own clothes label, called Cathy McGowan's Boutique, for a short while. For the first time, kids around the country were able to see all the latest styles and dances, presented by Patrick Kerr and the team, as they happened – not to mention great music. No Mod worth their salt would miss a single show.

During my research for this chapter I was looking back through some old *Ready Steady Go!* shows from 1965, and there dancing in the studio audience I saw two Mod girls, one of whom I recognised as a friend. She was wearing an Indianapolis 500 printed T-shirt and her mate had on a Moon Eyes drag racing equipment T-shirt.

I immediately emailed my friend, who is now a costume designer in Los Angeles, and learned that they had seen the American T-shirts advertised for mail order in a motor sport magazine, and so they wrote off for them. Up until this time, very little was known about drag racing in the UK, other than it was the fastest motor sport on the planet. There had been demonstrations on Brighton seafront the year before, but it took another year before it came properly to the UK, so these girls were in the true spirt of Mod, really ahead of their time!

The movement had its own language, walk or swagger, hairstyles, props and accessories, clubs, coffee bars and transport. By 1964, the numbers had grown enormously and inevitably the look had become diluted with more casual clothes being worn, and anyone who could afford a parka and scooter joined in.

Aggravation

During the heyday of Mod a number of English soul bands toured the main towns of England spreading the word. Bands, such as the Graham Bond Organisation, Steampacket, with Long John Baldry, Rod Stewart and Julie Driscoll, Georgie Fame and the Blue Flames, Zoot Money's Big Roll Band, Chris Farlowe and the Thunderbirds, Geno Washington's Ram Jam Band, The Who, and later the Small Faces, drew a large following, particularly of scooter Mods. They would congregate in town centres in groups, exchanging drugs and posing on their elaborate machines, much to the annoyance of the local biker gangs, who up until then had considered themselves kings of the road. The result was fighting between the new rivals on a small scale, which eventually led to mass Mod and Rocker riots at southern seaside towns during bank holidays in 1964. Much damage was caused, as the traditional holidaymakers' beaches became battlefields.

Above: 1. Chrome Zodiac Hermetic watch on chrome expanding strap, 1960, on tan leather driving gloves. This watch originally belonged to my father.

2. Steel comb, also useful as a weapon of defence, gilt framed sunglasses on pink Oxford cotton shirt by Ben Sherman, 1964-66, England.

Left: Cream striped linen blazer, John Michael, London, 1964-66. Pink and white striped Sea Island cotton polo shirt, John Smedley, England, mid 1960s.

Left: Fig 1. Mid blue and black three button striped linen blazer, Burlingtons, Ashoka Hotel, India, mid 1960s. Yellow rayon Italian-style knit shirt, Van Heusen, mid 1960s, USA. Yellow and white polka dot silk pocket handkerchief. Blue denim shrink-to-fit jeans, Levi's 501. Black and brown leather shoes, VIP, mid 1960s. This blazer was worn by Leo Gregory (Brian Jones) in the Brian Jones bio-pic *Stoned*, dir Stephen Woolley, 2005.

Fig 2. Olive green US Army M-51 parka, with wolf fur trim hood and fox tail detail, 1950s, USA. Red rayon polo shirt, mid 1960s, England. Black, white, red and yellow striped wool college scarf, St Andrews, Bute. Light grey straight leg slacks, Sta-Prest, mid 1960s, England. Black and white leather boxing boots, mid 1960s, England.

Fig 3. Tan suede jacket, Levi's Big E, mid 1960s, USA. Yellow, orange and brown paisley button-down collar shirt, Simon Stuart, mid 1960s, England. Black, grey and tan striped jeans, mid 1960s, England. Brown suede Italian style chukka boots, Chaparral Navarro, mid 1960s, England.

Right top: 1. Black leather staggered lace driving style shoes, mid 1960s, England.

2. Black leather multi-lace driving style shoes, mid 1960s, England.

3. Black leather driving style shoes, mid 1960s, England.

Right bottom: 1. Black leather lace up driving style shoes, Mayle, mid 1960s, England.

2. Black and brown leather driving style shoes, VIP, mid 1960s, England.

3. Black leather imitation whale hide chukka boots, with strap fastening, mid 1960s, England.

Above: Mod Girls, *Ready Steady Go!* TV Show, 1964.

Previous page and right: Fig 1. Bottle green three button tailored mohair jacket with ticket pocket and 12-inch centre vent, 1964-66, England. Red silk pocket handkerchief. Bottle green lambswool polo neck sweater. Brown moleskin straight leg trousers with raised stitching, mid 1960s, England. Brown suede almond toe brogue shoes, Denson, mid 1960s, England.

Fig 2. Camel wool skirt suit with a reefer style double-breasted jacket, Stromor, 1964-66, England. Brown patent leather almond toe strap shoes with a kitten heel, Sonate, mid 1960s, England.

Right: Fig 1. Maroon suede knee-length coat, mid 1960s, England. Heather wool sweater, Dalkeith, England. Beige, black, brown and green check wool hipster trousers, mid 1960s, England. Maroon wool socks. Beige suede and brown leather shoes, Hush Puppies, mid 1960s.

Fig 2. Bottle green suede coat, Oakleaf Leatherwear, mid 1960s, England. Light grey ribbed wool polo neck sweater. Ornate silver brooch with white stone. Grey and black check wool hipster trousers, mid 1960s, England. Silver leather strap shoes with black ball buttons, Raddys, England.

Fig 3. Red leather three button jacket, mid 1960s, England. Stone ribbed wool sweater, Hutchisons, mid 1960s, Scotland. Gilt leaf brooch pearls. Tan crepe skirt, Susan Small, mid 1960s, England. Black cotton knee socks. Black, white and red leather lace up bowling shoes, AMF, mid 1960s, USA.

Fig 4. Cream pigskin jacket with black trim, mid 1960s, England. Yellow wool sweater, Ballantyne of Peebles, mid 1960s, Scotland. Green and black slub silk skirt, mid 1960s, England. Black cotton knee socks. Black leather semi-point sneakers, Jay-Bill, England.

This group of girls illustrates a typical paired down Modernist approach to fashion at the time, and the so-called 'granny fashion' of wearing simple sweaters, costume jewellery and sensible shoes.

Above: Navy felt Blue Beat hat,
Christys, London.

Right: Fig 1. Camel wool sleeveless dropped
waist dress with horizontal and vertical
cream bands, 1964-1966, England. Chrome
elasticated arm band à la Cathy McGowan.
Tan and cream leather slingback shoes,
C Penata, mid 1960s, Italy.

Fig 2. Mid-blue double-breasted Trevira suit,
jacket has two eight-inch inverted side pleats,
Burton Tailoring, 1965-66, England. Grey
wool herringbone button-down collar shirt,
John Stephen for HIS Clothes, 1964-66,
England. Light grey silk pocket handkerchief.
Mid blue and black diagonal stripe silk tie,
mid 1960s, England. Black grainy leather
shoes with a centre seam and fringed golf
tongue, Eton Shoes, mid 1960s, England.

Fig 3. Black jersey sleeveless shift dress
with thick camel piping, Tom Jones, mid
1960s, Mayfair, London. Black and camel
patent leather lace up shoes, Fashion
Model, mid 1960s, England.

The End

By the mid 1960s the look had all but burnt itself out with the purists, who had seen the whole thing go mainstream very quickly. Something new and unacceptable had to be found. After a brief flirtation with Regency, dandy and military styles, a lot of Mods turned to the new Hippie culture, and a few like myself started wearing old gangster-style second-hand suits and lurid painted ties from the 1930s and 1940s.

Although not released until 1970, the seminal British film *Performance*, directed by Donald Cammell and Nicolas Roeg, clearly illustrates how incredibly exotic the Hippie culture, as depicted by stars Mick Jagger and Anita Pallenberg, was to the old guard of Mods, represented in this movie by the immaculate gangster Chas, played brilliantly by James Fox.

A few hardcore Mods got involved in the skinhead and suedehead scenes, while others were to keep the faith right through to the 1978 revival, which was directly inspired by the feature film *Quadrophenia*. This movie was also my introduction to the film business. At the time my partner and I were buying and selling original vintage clothes as a full-time job, and after initially being approached by the art director, the producers set on us as main supplier and style consultants for the production.

However, the later revivals seemed to be more concerned with emulating the commercial Carnaby Street looks that original purist 1960s Mods shunned, instead of trying to develop the style, which surely was the antithesis of the Mod ethos. But the legacy of this seminal movement can be seen in countless fashion looks to this day.

I personally was heartbroken when it all ended at a soul all-nighter in 1965. But the writing was on the wall, as the last record, 'I Got You Babe' by Sonny & Cher heralded in a Hippie revolution.

Above: *Quadrophenia*,
dir Franc Roddam, 1979.

Right: Fig 1. Navy nylon Pac-a-Mac,
Nicholls, mid 1960s, London. Olive and
blue plaid three button madras cotton blazer,
Stegan by Frank Price, mid 1960s, England.
Camel aertex T-shirt with navy neckband,
mid 1960s, England. Blue denim shrink-to-fit
jeans, Levi's 501, USA. Sand suede desert
boots, Clarks, mid 1960s, England.

7

THEIR SATANIC MAJESTIES

DRAG & DANDIES

LATE 1950s – LATE 1960s

'He looked me up and down while his thoughts came into focus, "Those clothes you wear," he said at last, "disgust me." And I hope they did! I had on precisely my full teenage drag that would enrage him – the grey pointed alligator casuals, the pink neon pair of ankle crepe nylon-stretch, my Cambridge blue glove-fit jeans, a vertical-striped happy shirt revealing my lucky neck-charm on its chain, and the Roman-cut short-arse jacket just referred to, not to mention my wrist identity jewel, and my Spartan warrior hair-do.'

Absolute Beginners, Colin MacInnes, 1958.

Absolute Beginners is a wonderful portrayal of Soho nightlife in the late 1950s, and the colourful teenage drag that MacInnes pictures so vividly in his book would have more than likely been found in Bill Green's seminal menswear shop Vince.

Green started out as a stage portrait photographer, but by the mid 1940s he had gained a reputation for photographing wrestlers and muscle boys for male study magazines under the pseudonym 'Vince'. Green had recognised a desperate need for interesting men's posing attire, and as none existed at the time, he began making his own. He soon started a busy mail order service for his mainly gay clientele. In 1952, he visited Paris and saw lots of young men who were wearing tight black jeans and black polo-neck sweaters. With nothing like this look in England, he decided that he should expand into casual outerwear. In 1954, he opened Vince Man's Shop in Newburgh Street, Soho, London. His business thrived, selling the style that he had been so inspired by in Paris.

Brightly coloured jeans, T-shirts, shirts and jumpers in pink, purple, yellow and green were placed alongside his famous posing wear. The more outrageous the design and unusual the fabric, the more his customers loved it. Shirts in satin, and jackets in velvet, vinyl and leather were much sought after.

A young Sean Connery modelled clothes for Vince before landing the role of James Bond, and as word spread rapidly through showbiz and music circles, soon many celebrities began to buy their clothes there. The shop became a haven for adventurous dressers who came in search of Green's distinctly youthful style. Even though the clothes being sold there were considered quite effeminate by most men at that stage, they were really ahead of their time, and actually more reflective of the American teenage styles of the day.

By the mid 1950s, Soho had espresso bars with jukeboxes springing up everywhere, and one of the most exciting haunts for young people to hang out at was the 2i's Coffee Bar in Old Compton Street. The 2i's had become an important venue for new rock 'n' roll stars to debut at and Tommy Steele, who was among them, became one of England's earliest pop idols. Another star, Terry Dene (who bore a strong resemblance to the American film star James Dean, both facially and in the way he dressed), was one of a growing number of young working-class kids who found instant success in the early days of pop. Teenagers wanted to dress like this new breed of rock 'n' roll stars, just as earlier generations had done with jazz singers and movie stars.

Previous page: *If....*
dir Lindsay Anderson, 1968.

Above: Eden Kane models
a mohair sweater, 1960.

Right: Black cotton fishnet top, silk leopard
print scarf Philippe Monet, silver scarf ring,
black leather belt with metal studs, beige wool
mix peg top trousers, mid 1950s, England.

Left and below: Fig 1. Tan leather jacket with distinctive button grouping, Vince, early 1960s, London. Black and white striped cotton matelot top, Beat Beat, mid 1980s, London. Pink mohair trousers, 1960s, USA. Peach suede 1960s style winkle-picker shoes.

Left: Fig 2. Pale blue PVC top, Melda Continental Leisurewear, early 1960s, England. Black and white striped cotton matelot top. Black and white early 1960s style tweed trousers with black trim. Black leather winkle-picker shoes with strap fastening, Denson, early 1960s, London.

Right: Fig 1. Blue linen collarless jacket, Fox, London, early 1960s. White tab collar shirt with blue polka dots, Wemblex, early 1960s, England. White cord Levi's, USA. Navy and red elastic snake belt, 1960s, England.

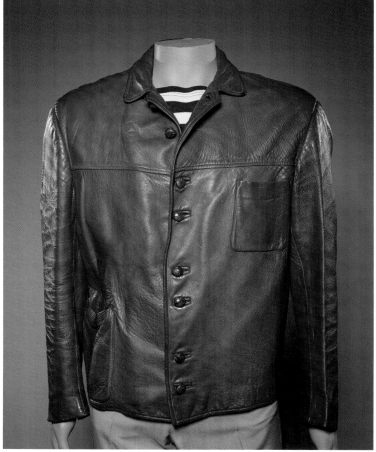

Carnaby Street

An astute young Scotsman called John Stephen picked up on this fan-like adoration while he was working as a salesman at Vince in 1956. Stephen also quickly recognised the potential for a shop like Vince to capture a more commercial market, and by 1957 he had left Green and moved to a small room in Beak Street, Soho, to set up on his own business. He began making and selling his own designs, and later that year, with £300 he had saved up, Stephen decided to rent a shop just around the corner from Vince on Carnaby Street, calling it His Clothes. He never looked back – within ten years Stephen's astute observations and business head had turned him into a millionaire.

The shop was modelled on a South-of-France-style boutique with clothes hanging outside, and the windows, like the interior, were awash with colour. His Clothes had loud pop music playing and stocked the very latest in sharp English, American, and 'Continental style' casual wear, bright-coloured jeans, sweaters, shirts, Italian-style winkle-picker shoes, and bum-freezer suits, and with these fashionable items, the shop immediately had a captive audience. The opening of His Clothes was also very timely as it coincided with BBC launching their very first television pop music programme, *Six-Five Special*. Prior to this, the best way for kids to keep in touch with the pop music scene was by listening to Radio Luxembourg or the AFN (American Forces Network) radio station based in Germany.

Left: Fig 1. Black leather coat, early 1960s, German. Grey cotton polo neck sweater with dark grey check repeat pattern, early 1960s, England. Pale grey trousers, Sta-Prest, 1960s, England. Black leather 1960s style winkle-picker shoes with red saddle stitching, Shelleys, 1980s, London.

Fig 2. Brown and bronze check collarless jacket, John Collier, early 1960s. London. Navy and red polka dot giraffe neck tab collar shirt, Marvic, early 1960s London. Black wool trousers, early 1960s, England. Black leather Chelsea boots, 1960s, England.

Fig 3. Navy wool reefer coat, with knitted shawl collar, Jaeger, 1960s, England. White cotton tab collar shirt with blue polka dot print, Wemblex. Black wool trousers, early 1960s, England. Black leather side lace winkle shoes, early 1960s, England.

Fig 4. Black and white Donegal tweed jacket with black PVC trim, Gamp Ferris, early 1960s, London. White cotton roll-neck sweater. Bronze Roman head medallion, early 1960s, England. Black PVC 1960s style trousers. Black mock snakeskin fine point winkle-pickers, Johnsons, 1980s, London.

The clothes Stephen stocked, although similar to Vince, were even more risqué in colour and style and had cheaper price tags. Trade flourished, and two more menswear shops called Donis and Domino Male, opened in Carnaby Street later that same year. By 1958, millions were watching television's latest pop showcase *Oh Boy!*, and Soho was buzzing with activity. This was largely due to pop music impresario Larry Parnes who was also based there, and whose growing stable of pop stars included Marty Wilde, Billy Fury, Johnny Gentle, Vince Eager and Duffy Power. These and many others were now seen on TV wearing styles of casual clothing similar to those that Vince, His Clothes and Donis had been promoting, and Stephen's ideas were becoming even bigger. By 1961, other shops had moved to Carnaby Street, and Stephen had opened four more shops there in direct competition with each other, for his main ambition was to open more boutiques than anyone else. The area was now becoming well known as a centre for modern menswear.

In 1962, Sally Tuffin and Marion Foale opened a girls' boutique on Carnaby Street, where they introduced their 'Fun' range of clothes, which included a creative approach to the use of lace curtains. Short dresses made from the fabric sailed out of the shop and wholesale orders flooded in. These two important new designers had left the RCA the year before declaring, '*We, don't want to be chic; we just want to be ridiculous.*'

Stephen capitalised on the power of celebrity and used popular British boxer Billy Walker in a promotional campaign. Large photographs of the macho boxer wearing pink denim slacks, striped matelot shirts and a variety of other designs adorned the windows of Stephen's wild shops. It was as if Walker had given men a stamp of approval to now wear such colours as pink and purple. However the real turning point in Stephen's career came when Cliff Richard was seen on national television wearing one of his furry mohair-style sweaters. Sales boomed and other pop stars, such as Adam Faith, became customers.

The nation was gripped by Merseybeat fever, and the Beatles, in particular, with their mop-top haircuts, became teenage style icons. Dressed in collarless suits made by Soho tailor Dougie Millings, which had been inspired by Pierre Cardin's original 'cylinder' look from 1960, they wore gingham tab-collar shirts, knitted ties and Cuban heel boots, made by Anello and Davide in Drury Lane. The boots, also known as 'Chelsea boots' and 'Beatle boots', became so popular that every boy wanted them, and on Saturdays long queues would form of teenagers who were desperate to buy them.

Above: Carnaby Street Mods, London, 1964.

Left: Fig 1. Black and white Donegal tweed jacket with black PVC trim, Gamp Ferris, early 1960s, London. White cotton roll-neck sweater. Bronze Roman head medallion, early 1960s, England. Black PVC 1960s style trousers. Black mock snakeskin fine point winkle-pickers, Johnsons, 1980s, London.

Above: Amanda Lear, Nigel Waymouth and friends, London, 1967.

Right: Green brocade linen Nehru style jacket, Enny Pinckert, mid 1960s, California. Green and red floral chiffon pointed scarf.

In 1964, Radio Caroline, the first pirate radio station, filled the airwaves with non-stop pop music, and BBC TV began its long-running chart show *Top of the Pops*. The Kinks, who started out wearing hunting pink jackets and giraffe-necked polka-dot shirts with a penny round collar, in many ways epitomised the Street's ever changing fashions. Carnaby Street had begun as a great source of clothes for Mods, and many worked in the shops themselves, but as the Street gained more and more publicity, top Mods would avoid it like the plague, as they considered the clothes were far too commercial.

That same year, the new bad boys of rock 'n' roll, the Rolling Stones, stole the limelight, and they too were photographed wearing Carnaby Street clothes. But the suede and tweed three-button jackets, high-neck tab-collar shirts, black leather coats and waistcoats, tight black stretch-jersey trousers and Chelsea boots gave them a much lower key, art school kind of style, quite similar to early Mods. The Stones' manager, Andrew Loog Oldham, proclaimed that pop was taking the place of religion and the Beatles, who had just released their first film *A Hard Day's Night*, were gods.

With such high demand for new styles, the accent soon shifted again, with designers looking to the old British Empire and the East for inspiration. Pretty soon brightly coloured Nehru jackets, worn with original 1930s pointed scarves, slim floral ties, shocking-pink hipsters and art nouveau buckled belts, became all the rage.

Around the same time, several young bucks were spotted rummaging around junk shops and street markets in London, looking for Victorian and Edwardian frock coats and costumes, which could still be found relatively cheaply. *Vogue* magazine actually ran an article entitled 'The Attic Dressers, 1965 Dandies' about the phenomenon. In it they reported that '*a few bright lads, home from 6th form or university for the holidays, got bored with wearing dirty jeans. Without the funds for Carnaby Street they looked for, and are still finding, grandpa's frock coat and Dad's wedding outfit.*'

This ushered in a new decadent period of Regency and dandy styles for men, with The Rolling Stones, and Brian Jones in particular, epitomising the look. Chelsea became the place to find it, with shops such as Hung On You and its art-deco-style rising sun sign, and Granny Takes a Trip, which stocked Victorian frock coats, military tunics and vintage couture dresses as well as their own new designs. Also popular were the latest wide kipper ties with 1930s-inspired prints created by Mr Fish, and men began wearing elaborate costume jewellery. Interest in old uniforms grew and, in 1966, an emporium called I Was Lord Kitchener's Valet opened on Portobello Road,

stocking antique military uniforms and bright-red guards' jackets with a full regalia of medals and ribbons, which of course kids and pop stars loved but the establishment took as a bitter insult. As a backdrop to all this, the V&A held an inspirational Aubrey Beardsley exhibition that year, which influenced everything from fabric prints to shop interiors.

Brian Jones was beginning to gain quite a reputation for his outrageous antics, and one infamous photo shoot for a German magazine caused particular outrage, as it pictured Jones dressed in a full SS uniform treading on a toy doll while posing alongside his German girlfriend Anita Pallenberg. As Jones explained afterwards, *'Really, I mean with all that long hair in a Nazi uniform, couldn't people see that it was a satirical thing?'* Years later Anita was said to have commented, *'It was naughty! But what the hell! He looked good in an SS uniform!'*

In 1967, The Beatles' *Sgt. Pepper's Lonely Hearts Club Band* album cover did masses to sanction antique uniforms as fashion, as did the movie *Far From the Madding Crowd*, 1967, directed by John Schlesinger and starring Terence Stamp. And in 1968, radical director Lindsay Anderson released the public school satire *If....* starring Malcolm McDowell, whose character sought to rebel against this privileged system. The film is a great example of a bygone style of traditional attire that was influencing the new crop of attic dressers and dandies.

Left: Fig 1. Yellow cotton tunic jacket with gilt buttons, Mercatores Via Manzoni, mid 1960s, Italy. Navy, red, and pale blue crepe pointed scarf 1930s, England. Red, gold and blue mid 1960s style striped velvet trousers. Green leather slip-on shoes with side buckle, Verde, mid 1960s, Italy.

Fig 2. Cream and gold brocade Nehru jacket, Burlingtons, mid 1960s, Bombay. Gold crushed velvet trousers, mid 1960s, England. Black leather Chelsea boots, mid 1960s, England.

Fig 3. Brown wool smock dress, Mary Quant, mid 1960s, London. Yellow patent slingback shoes with daisy decoration, Elliott Collection Art Nouveau, mid 1960s, England.

Fig 4. Green brocade linen Nehru style jacket, Enny Pinckert, mid 1960s, California. Green and red floral chiffon pointed scarf. Deep gold crushed velvet trousers, mid 1960s, England. Yellow leather slip-on shoes with side buckle, Verde, mid 1960s, Italy.

The Chelsea Set

As Carnaby Street had become the centre for men's street fashion, so the Kings Road in London's Chelsea became the women's wear equivalent. One of the first to start the extravaganza was Mary Quant, who in 1955 along with her boyfriend, Alexander Plunket Greene and partner Archie McNair, opened the Bazaar boutique close to the Markham Arms pub. McNair had just opened Britain's first coffee bar, called The Fantasy, which was also on the Kings Road and a meeting place for the 'Chelsea Set', in which the partners were also involved.

The Chelsea Set was largely made up from young white upper-class men and women, public schoolboys, debutantes and bohemians, who had recently moved to the area. They were renowned for their wild parties, to which they invited celebrities, members of society, artists, jazz musicians and well-known criminals. When not holding parties, they would congregate at the Markham Arms, Finch's pub and the Chelsea Arts Club.

None of the partners knew the first thing about selling clothes, so to them a shop was quite a gamble. Quant had previously studied at art school and worked for a short time at a couture milliners, where she would spend several days trimming a single hat for a rich client. This experience frustrated Quant, who believed that fashion should be available to everyone, especially young girls, and at prices they could afford. Quant also considered the French couturiers, who pretty much dictated seasonal styles and fabrics, to be out-dated. She wanted Bazaar to stock clothes that were absolutely twentieth century in design.

> 'To me a fashionable woman is one who is ahead of the current rage. She must have a personal style, be aware of it and wear those clothes that emphasise it. A fashionable woman wears clothes; the clothes don't wear her. Clothes should live, breathe and move with the wearer.'
>
> Mary Quant, *Quant By Quant*, 1966.

After initially being inspired by fashions of the 1920s and 1930s, Quant began to experiment with new designs that broke the rules, such as knickerbockers for girls and balloon dresses. She used clashing fabrics and patterns and put large spots and checks together. She also caused an outrage by dropping the waistline on dresses, and losing it altogether on a pinafore dress and her version of the 'sac' dress, which had originally been created by Christian Dior for his final collection in 1957. Her unique approach to women's fashion attracted a new generation of bright young things, who loved the simplicity and stylish lines of her clothes.

Above: Terence Stamp, *Far From The Madding Crowd*, dir John Schlesinger, 1967.

Left: Fig 1. Red wool Coldstream guards jacket, England. Silver MBE medal, England. Black and white patent belt with brass Native American Indian head buckle, mid 1960s, USA. Black and grey wool mourning trousers, mid 1960s, England.

Fig 2. White and red PVC collarless raincoat, Alligator by Mary Quant, mid 1960s, England. White PVC boots, mid 1960s, England.

Fig 3. Black wool Hussars jacket with frogging, England. Gilt fringed epaulettes, Turin Italy. Black, yellow, purple and white mid 1960s style striped wool trousers, England.

Fig 4. Red and white PVC collarless raincoat, Alligator by Mary Quant, mid 1960s, England. White and clear PVC boots, mid 1960s, England.

Above: Red wool Coldstream guards jacket, England. Silver MBE medal, England. Black and white patent belt with brass Native American Indian head buckle, mid 1960s, USA.

Right: Fig 1. Brown, yellow and white striped wool blazer, Standen & Co, 1920s, Oxford. Yellow botany wool polo neck sweater. Buff cotton jeans, mid 1960s, USA. Navy and cream leather correspondent shoes, Florsheim Lightweights, mid 1960s, USA. Straw boater, Olney, Luton.

Fig 2. Grey cotton smock dress, mid 1960s, England. Cream patent T-bar granny shoes, Elliott Jeunesse West One, mid 1960s, England.

Fig 3. Black wool blazer with rust binding, Lord John, mid 1960s, Carnaby Street, London. Black and rust striped cotton mid 1960s style trousers, England. Black leather Chelsea Boots, mid 1960s, England.

By the end of the decade, Bazaar had become a success, with its continuous party atmosphere and wild window displays that were always attracting crowds of bemused onlookers. Many of Quant's designs would sell out the same day they entered the shop.

Mary Quant led the way, and others followed in the wake of her success. One person who she claims greatly helped to develop the 'cult', was her 16-year-old assistant-cum-window dresser Andrew Loog Oldham, who at 19 became the Rolling Stones' first manager.

'What a great many people still don't realize is that the Look isn't just the garments you wear. It's the way you put your make-up on, the way you do your hair, the sort of stockings you choose, the way you walk and stand; even the way you smoke your fag. All these are a part of the same "feeling".'

Mary Quant, *Quant By Quant*, 1966.

In 1962, the first issue of *The Sunday Times Magazine* ran a feature on her clothes, modelled by Jean Shrimpton and photographed by David Bailey. That same year, she introduced trouser suits for girls, which became very popular, especially with Mods, who were all about unisex fashion. Quant was now exporting what she termed 'the Look' to America; this included a full range of accessories and mix-and-match separates. And in Paris, she promoted her new culottes, and her Wet' collection made entirely from brightly coloured PVC.

With skirt lengths getting shorter, 1963 was declared the year of the leg with the mini-skirt more popular than ever. Hair stylist Vidal Sassoon created a new short angular haircut, called the 'Bob' to complement 'the Look', and a new music and fashion-fuelled TV series, called *Ready Steady Go!*, had also just begun. Introduced by Mod heroine Cathy McGowan, who was often dressed from head to toe in Quant clothes, *Ready Steady Go!* did much to ensure the success of Quant and other Modernist fashion designers during its three-year run.

Also that year, a new fashion designer called Barbara Hulanicki, and her partner Stephen Fitz-Simon, launched their Biba mail-order business. This saw the beginnings of one of the most fashionable 1960s labels. With styles changing daily, the market was expanding, and Biba aimed at the highly lucrative, mass teenage girl sector, offering them even cheaper fashionable clothes than Quant. The orders flooded in, and as a direct result, in 1964, they opened a small Biba boutique in Abingdon Road just off High Street Kensington. The shop was constantly packed with cheap clothes and dolly birds.

By 1965, crochet dresses, tops and skirts were all the rage, and fashion designer John Bates introduced bold black-and-white op art prints and dramatic leather catsuits to the costumes of Diana Rigg in the latest television series of *The Avengers*.

In 1966, Ossie Clark and Alice Pollock, both ex-RCA students, opened their upmarket fashion boutique Quorum, which attracted a new clientele that included wealthy pop stars. Biba moved to a larger shop on Kensington Church Street and Hulanicki, like Quant, promoted a complete Biba girl look. The new shop had been designed to appear more like a discotheque or club than a clothes shop, with its loud pop music, dim lighting, dark wood, art nouveau-style screens and potted palm plants in Victorian jardinières – the shop caused quite a stir. Coats were casually hung on bentwood hat-stands alongside feather boas, wide-brim, floppy felt hats, and tiny dresses with high tight armholes and short flared skirts. And every girl bought a pair of matching high-leg boots in suede or canvas. Customers would often wait for hours to see new deliveries. This coordinated style, combined with Hulanicki's unique sense of colour, which featured grey, prune, brown and plum, and also came with a range of matching cosmetics, proved to be a massive success, and alongside the Hippie look, it would be a mainstay of high street style for the remainder of the 1960s.

Right: Fig 1. Black velvet waistcoat, mid 1960s, England. Gilt watch chain. White cotton shirt, mid 1960s, England. Red silk tie. Grey and black striped mourning trousers, mid 1960s, England. Black leather Edwardian style boots, mid 1960s, England.

Fig 2. Black silk organza mini-dress with white collar and coin cuff links, Diorling by Christian Dior, mid 1960s, Paris. Black leather shoes with white leather tongue, Jegas at Saks Fifth Avenue, mid 1960s, USA.

Fig 3. Black cotton lace mini-dress, Shubette, mid 1960s, London. Black patent granny shoes with side buckle, Camalots QualiCraft, mid 1960s, USA.

Fig 4. Edwardian frock coat, 1905-14, England. White cotton shirt, mid 1960s, England. Red and white Beardsley influenced floral silk tie, Take Six, mid 1960s, London. Black wool trousers, mid 1960s, England. Black leather Chelsea boots, mid 1960s, England.

Left: Fig 1. Red and black crepe wrap-over mini-dress, Marion Foale & Sally Tuffin, mid 1960s, England. Silver chain and ribbon with shark's tooth and leaf charms.

Fig 2. Black wool Nazi SS replica uniform with full regalia. This uniform was worn by Leo Gregory (Brian Jones) in the Brian Jones bio-pic *Stoned*, dir Stephen Woolley, 2005.

Right: Fig 1. Black wool mourning coat, England. White cotton wing collar shirt, England. Black and red striped silk tie, Austin Reed, mid 1960s, England. Red and gold cotton brocade waistcoat, England. Black and grey striped mourning trousers, mid 1960s, England. Black leather Chelsea boots, mid 1960s, England.

Fig 2. Grey silk organza dress, Young Edwardian by Arpeja, mid 1960s, California. Silver and gold lurex lace up shoes, Flings, mid 1960s, England.

Left: Fig 1. Red cotton lace mini-dress, Betsey Johnson for Paraphernalia, mid 1960s, USA. Alloy slave necklace with coin detail, mid 1960s, England. Black leather platform knee boots, mid 1960s, England.

Fig 2. Black and white striped mid 1960s style wool suit, England. White shirt, mid 1960s, England. Black and red silk polka dot tie, mid 1960s, England. Black and red silk floral pocket handkerchief. Black leather Chelsea boots, mid 1960s, England.

Above: Grey and black herringbone suit, Granny Takes a Trip, 1967. Green check silk frill front shirt, mid 1960s. Brooch with amber stones in a gilt mount.

Left: Grey and black herringbone suit, Granny Takes a Trip, 1967. Green check silk frill front shirt, mid 1960s. Brooch with amber stones in a gilt mount. Black leather Beatle boots.

Right: Fig 1. Red floral wool mini-dress, mid 1960s, England. Brown suede knee boots, mid 1960s, England.

Fig 2. Bottle green suede fringed mid 1960s style jacket, England. Cream crepe frill front mid 1960s style shirt, England. Red and black silk swirl scarf, mid 1960s, England. Red jumbo cord mid 1960s style trousers. Tan leather belt with brass and glass stone decorated buckle. Alloy sunglasses with bug eye lens, mid 1960s, England. Mock snakeskin Cuban heel boots.

Below: Red jumbo cord mid 1960s style trousers. Tan leather belt with brass and glass stone decorated buckle. Alloy sunglasses with bug eye lens, mid 1960s, England.

Left: Fig 1. Navy chalk stripe jacket with velvet trim, Dandie Fashions, mid 1960s, England. White cotton frill front shirt, mid 1960s, England. Silver and glass brooch with red and blue stones, 1920s. Blue mohair trousers, mid 1960s, England. Black Chelsea style boots, Florsheim, mid 1960s, USA.

Fig 2. Navy linen mini-dress with cream monogrammed kipper tie decoration, Miss Torrente, mid 1960s, Paris. Blue plastic bug eye sunglasses, mid 1960s, England. Black silk shoes with bows, Starlight Room, mid 1960s, England.

Right: Brian Jones and Keith Richards, London, 1967.

Left: 1. White lace cuffs. Carved ebony stick, African.

2. Navy chalk stripe jacket with velvet trim, Dandie Fashions, mid 1960s, England. White cotton frill front shirt, mid 1960s, England. Silver and glass brooch with red and blue stones, 1920s.

Right: Fig 1. Grey wool chalk stripe frock coat with black velvet trim, Lord John, mid 1960s, Carnaby Street. White lace stock, white lace cuffs. Silver starburst brooch, mid 1960s, England. Black wool trousers, mid 1960s, England. Black leather Chelsea boots with centre seam, mid 1960s, England. Carved ebony stick, African. This frock coat was worn by Leo Gregory (Brian Jones) in the Brian Jones bio-pic *Stoned*, dir Stephen Woolley, 2005.

Fig 2. Black and white satin mini-dress with Beardsley inspired paisley print, mid 1960s, England. Black leather belt, mid 1960s, England. Black ostrich feather boa. Black felt floppy hat, mid 1960s, England. Black suede platform knee boots, mid 1960s, England.

Left: Fig 1. Red cotton lace blouse, mid 1960s, England. Red ceramic lozenge necklace, Morocco. Black leather belt, mid 1960s, England. Purple suede mini-skirt, mid 1960s, England. Purple denim knee boots, Biba, mid 1960s, England. Purple ostrich feather boa.

Fig 2. Sand mohair suit with brown velvet collar, stage suit for soul singer Chris Farlowe, Aubrey Morris, mid 1960s, London. White and red cotton Art Nouveau print shirt, Revelation, mid 1960s, England. Burgundy and white leather correspondent shoes, Johnston & Murphy Aristocrat, mid 1960s, USA.

Left and right: Fig 3. Black, pink and gold paisley print polyester wrap mini-dress, Louis Caring, mid 1960s, London. Pink ostrich feather boa. Silver alloy square link chain belt, mid 1960s, England. Red felt floppy hat, mid 1960s, England. Brown suede and leather lace-up knee boots, mid 1960s, England.

8

COME TOGETHER

HIPPIES & BOHEMIANS

MID 1960S – EARLY 1970S

George Hanson: 'You know, this used to be a helluva good country. I can't understand what's gone wrong with it.'

Billy: 'Man, everybody got chicken, that's what happened. Hey, we can't even get into like, a second-rate hotel, I mean, a second-rate motel, you dig? They think we're gonna cut their throat or somethin'. They're scared, man.'

George Hanson: 'They're not scared of you. They're scared of what you represent to 'em.'

Billy: 'Hey, man. All we represent to them, man, is somebody who needs a haircut.'

George Hanson: 'Oh, no. What you represent to them is freedom.'

Easy Rider, dir Dennis Hopper, 1969.

In 1961, a 20-year-old folk singer called Bob Dylan, from Minnesota, travelled east to meet his hero, the legendary Woody Guthrie. Dylan had made a huge impression on all who had heard him play and within a few months of meeting Guthrie, his greatest influence, he had received rave reviews from New York's noted folk music critics and was busily working on his first album. His talent as a writer, singer and musician was quite extraordinary. He had learnt the power of words from the gurus of the Beat generation and coupled them with a unique sound that encompassed folk, blues and country music. Dylan's extremely poignant lyrics, and his ability to cross over musical styles, pierced the conscience of a post-War generation who cared that the world should be saved and have a peaceful future. He left no stone unturned: love, war, politics, religion, racism and drugs, each fell victim to his cutting tongue. His following, which had grown steadily through the early 1960s, suddenly multiplied after he played his first all-electric concert to a shocked audience at the 1965 Newport Folk Festival. He also appeared on stage wearing a leather jacket, which was seen as a further endorsement of his anti-establishment beliefs.

Previous page: eden ahbez, Los Angeles, 1948.

In the early 1940s eden ahbez moved from New York to Los Angeles, and became one of the first to embrace an alternative hippie lifestyle. He was vegetarian who studied mysticism, and for several years he and his family camped beneath the letter L of the Hollywood sign in Los Angeles. He also played piano and bongos at the famous Eutropheon raw food restaurant in Laurel Canyon, whose customers were known as nature boys.

During 1948 he approached crooner Nat King Cole with a composition he had written called 'Nature Boy'. Cole had a No 1 hit with the song, which has since become a jazz classic. During the mid 1960s, ahbez had a considerable influence on California hippies; the Beach Boys' Brian Wilson and folk singer Donovan were among his many followers.

Right: Fig 1. White cotton muslin shirt and trousers, India. White cotton shirt, mid 1960s, England. Cream red and black psychedelic print cotton tie, mid 1960s, England. Baubles, leis and bells, India. Tapestry woven tote bag mid 1960s, India.

Fig 2. Purple shot silk waistcoat, mid 1960s, England. Brown cotton shirt Dan-Haitu Spirits, mid 1960s, USA. Ethnic beads and braids. Brown leather belt, brown cord jeans, mid 1960s, England. Leather strap boots, YSL, mid 1960s, Paris.

Fig 3. Green, black and cream woven floral poncho, mid 1960s, England. Scottish silver plaid brooch with quartz stone. Beads and bells. Sunflower yellow polyester bell sleeve blouse, Cheeky Knits by Lady Manhattan, mid 1960s, USA. Red suede mini-skirt with black fringe detail, mid 1960s, England. Black leather knee boots, mid 1960s, England.

Fig 4. Black satin paisley print gambler's waistcoat, mid 1960s, England. White cotton seersucker roll-neck shirt, The Original Turnbull's Turtle, Turnbull & Asser, mid 1960s, London. Black and white Navajo beadwork necklace. Grey and black herringbone tweed trousers, Granny Takes a Trip, mid 1960s, London. Black leather Chelsea boots, mid 1960s, England.

Fig 5. Cream, brown and orange Cowichan style cardigan, mid 1960s, USA. Brown, rust, green silk, side button shirt, London Docks, mid 1960s, England. Blue denim jeans, Wrangler, mid 1960s, USA. Black leather Chelsea boots, mid 1960s, England.

Above: Allen Ginsberg and friends
circumambulating the Polo Fields at Golden
Gate Park during the Gathering of the Tribes for
a Human Be-In, January 14, 1967, ©Lisa Law.

His influence as a writer and musician quickly became massive, and countless bands recorded his songs. To the Hippie movement throughout the world he was a born leader, and everywhere he went he was treated like the new Messiah, and the king of counterculture.

Around the time that Dylan was starting out on his journey, the city of San Francisco, which for many years had been a meeting place and catalyst for Beats, bohemians and artists, was hit with a huge influx of cultural activity through the new Hippie movement.

From early in the 1960s, psychologist Timothy Leary had been experimenting with the mind-altering effects of magic mushrooms. In 1962, he was introduced to an hallucinogenic drug called Lysergic Acid Diethylamide 25, in short LSD or acid. Dr Albert Hofmann in Basel, Switzerland, had accidentally discovered the drug in 1943, while he was researching a cure for the common migraine. Leary raved about his experiences with LSD, which he shared with, among others, the Beat authors William Burroughs, Ken Kesey and Ken Babbs. Burroughs, author of *Naked Lunch*, 1959, had already spent a great deal of his life discovering, indulging and enthusing over all types of drugs with his close friend and lover, Beat poet Allen Ginsberg, and each extolled LSD's powerful visionary virtues. Kesey, author of the 1962 novel *One Flew Over the Cuckoo's Nest*, had also been one of earliest people to experiment with the drug.

Further

In 1964 Kesey and Babbs gathered together a group of friends, who called themselves the 'Merry Pranksters', and set off on a legendary trip across America in a psychedelically painted 1939 International Harvester school bus. The bus, which they named 'Furthur', was driven by Neal Cassady, a close friend of Beat author Jack Kerouac. It was laden down with film and audio equipment, jazz instruments, loud speakers and large amounts of LSD. Practically the whole journey was carried out under the influence of the drug, and many hours were recorded on film as they travelled through 'inner space'. Along the route they picked up a teenage runaway and painted her entire body in the colours of the bus, and in New York they threw a party to which both Ginsberg and Kerouac turned up.

Throughout the trip, the Pranksters wore a variety of Beatnik-style striped shirts; ethnic beads and embroidered hats; white boiler suits with a large blue Captain America style roundel appliqued on the back (containing a white central star symbol surrounded by 12 smaller stars) and a blue square pocket containing white star on the front breast; and, at other times, Halloween and jester costumes.

'Going through the streams of southern Alabama in late June and Kesey rises up from out of the comic books and becomes Captain Flag. He puts on a Pink kilt, like a mini skirt, and pink socks and patent-leather shoes and pink sunglasses and wraps an American flag around his head like a big turban and holds it in place with an arrow through the back of it and gets on top of the bus roaring through Alabama and starts playing the flute at people passing by.'

The Electric Kool-Aid Acid Test, Tom Wolfe, 1968.

What took place on that mystical journey was a highly symbolic and important act, for it not only threw the doors wide-open to a whole new culture, but also paid great homage to its original founders.

'The torch had been passed from the Beat to the Psychedelic, with Cassady as the driver, the tour guide, the swing man, foot in both eras, the flame passing from Kerouac to Kesey.'

'The Intrepid Traveler', Ken Babbs, 1990.

On his return to San Francisco, Kesey organised a series of legendary parties known as 'Acid Tests'. One of the most famous was held at a Grateful Dead concert in the Avalon Ballroom, San Francisco. Here Kesey's Pranksters and a group of Hippies mixed large quantities of LSD into dustbins full of soft drinks, and dished it out to a willing audience. Around the same time, Timothy Leary set up the Castalia Foundation, handing out licenses and certificates to all who were willing to try the drug. Leary proclaimed that LSD should be freely available and everyone should 'turn on, tune in, drop out'. It was claimed that the drug's effects were so mind-expanding and fantastic that they enabled the user to transcend normal life and enter a beautiful carefree existence.

Leary referred to the total experience as a taking a 'trip', but very little was mentioned of the bad trips that could be occasionally experienced. For it was 'all too beautiful'. LSD was finally made illegal in October 1966, but by this time illicit manufacture of the drug had begun in earnest, and its psychedelic effects were seen everywhere, most notably in music, fashion, art and literature. During that year, the Haight-Ashbury area of San Francisco became the centre of the LSD universe and thousands of Hippies flocked there to take a trip.

Early in 1967, the *San Francisco Oracle* announced – 'A gathering of the Tribes for a Human Be-In' to be held at Golden Gate Park in January. The Be-In had been set up initially to provide a platform for people to protest against the recent banning of LSD, but it also became a great way of introducing some key and quite revolutionary ideas from the new counterculture.

Some 20,000 Hippies turned up to hear Leary speak and Ginsberg, dressed in white robes, flowers and beads, read poetry. Big Brother and the Holding Company, the Grateful Dead, Jefferson Airplane and several other bands supplied the music. The event would also be a preamble for the incredible Summer of Love that was about to get into full swing. This kicked off in June with the very orderly Monterey Pop Festival, which had been organised by John Phillips of the Mamas & the Papas. The three-day event attracted many members of Hippie royalty, from Janis Joplin, the Byrds and Jimi Hendrix, who all played, to Brian Jones and Nico, who sat in the audience.

Wholly Communion

Antique dealers Adrian Emmerton and Vernon Lambert had a stall at an antiques market in Marylebone, London, specialising in art nouveau, in 1962. But they started to become very interested in period clothes after coming across a collection of 1920s Chanel dresses. By 1964, they had moved to the Chelsea Antiques Market on the Kings Road and opened one of the first period-clothes shops. They hired socialite and ideas person Ulla Larsson to manage the shop and did a roaring trade in Regency-style coats, Victorian and Edwardian frock coats, art nouveau shawls and 1920s flapper dresses; Twiggy worked for them part time before being discovered. Under Larsson's influence they were dyeing 1930s and 1940s collarless shirts, Victorian nightshirts and old white bell-bottom sailors' trousers in bright colours, along with tie-dye T-shirts which sold really well to the trendier set; word soon spread to the pop fraternity. At the time, along with the Pheasantry, Larsson's Chelsea flat was *the* hang out for Hippie royalty, so much so that she was name-checked by Turner (Mick Jagger) in *Performance*, 1970.

In June 1965, the International Poetry Incarnation was held at the Royal Albert Hall in London, attracting poets from the English alternative arts scene, such as Pete Brown, and the American Beat poet Allen Ginsberg. Among its packed audience, several groups of young people carrying joss sticks and flowers and wearing an unusual assortment of second-hand clothes really stood out: this is thought to be the earliest sighting of British kids dressing in elements of the Hippie style. The event was filmed by Peter Whitehead and released as a documentary called *Wholly Communion*.

A few American organisers from the festival stayed on in London to help create a new underground scene, which began with a series of events known as 'Spontaneous Underground', which were held at the Marquee Club on Sunday afternoons. More small happenings followed throughout 1966, and these expanded and culminated in a launch party for a new underground magazine,

IT (or *International Times*), in October at the Roundhouse, Chalk Farm. The party attracted over 2,000 people, many in fancy dress and under the influence of LSD, who turned up to see Soft Machine and Pink Floyd play. Music photographer and stylist Karl Ferris projected one of the first-known oil-based 'liquid light shows' at the party.

Ferris had recently been on a photo assignment in Ibiza where he had discovered The Fool, a Dutch duo of psychedelic fashion designers and artists, Marijke Koger and Simon Posthuma. Totally inspired by their work, he took photos of them, which later appeared in *The Sunday Times Magazine*. This was the first time psychedelic fashion and photography had ever been featured in a British magazine.

Invited to London, they designed for leading Hippie bands of the time, such as the Move, the Incredible String Band and Cream. They also worked with the Beatles for a couple of years, and in 1969 when the Beatles' Apple Boutique opened on Baker Street, The Fool painted its amazing psychedelic exterior and interior, and designed an extraordinary range of expensive clothes for the Boutique, most of which were stolen at the opening as there was no security.

'All of the people on earth are forced to come together now and this expresses itself even in fashion. Our ideas come from every country – India, China, Russia, Turkey and from the sixteenth to the twenty-first centuries. There's a bit of everything.'

'The Fools Paradise', Marijke Koger, *Observer Magazine*, 3 December 1967.

At the end of 1966, Vernon Lambert had come back from India with rolls of elaborately printed silk fabric to make into dresses, shirts and scarves. The partners also bought up hundreds of beads and bells, items of fancy dress and tie-dye, three-button granddad vests. At the weekends, long queues of youngsters and pop personalities formed outside, all clamouring to buy any article of the new Hippie look, whether it fit or not.

Happenings

A new underground club, called UFO, opened at 31 Tottenham Court Road at the end of 1966. It became the most famous haunt for followers of the counterculture until it closed after less than a year in October 1967. Artists Michael English and Nigel Waymouth (of Granny Takes a Trip fame), were among Britain's leading designers of psychedelic graphics, and together had a company called Hapshash and the Coloured Coat, which not only produced posters for the UFO club but also important

bands of the time, such as the Jimi Hendrix Experience, Soft Machine and the Move. In 1968, they made an LP record together with a group of friends and the band Spooky Tooth. The album, in bright red vinyl, was called *Hapshash & The Coloured Coat featuring The Human Host & The Heavy Metal Kids*. Waymouth had taken the name Heavy Metal Kids from William Burroughs' famous novel *Naked Lunch*.

Throughout 1967, London became a huge melting pot of world cultures, with Afghan, Moroccan, Indian, Tibetan and Native American cultures all being plundered for original garments and ideas.

The past became the present, and countless Hippies scoured markets like Portobello Road and old junk shops, looking for unusual antique garments, which they would coordinate with the wealth of new suits, shirts, dresses, tops and skirts being made up from ethnic cloths by boutiques hoping to capitalise on the look.

The early Hippies were quite fashion orientated, taking their lead from the London scene, but as the look evolved and became more of a lifestyle, many individuals either dropped out, or spread their wings and went in search of even more exotic clothes and cheap drugs along the Hippie trail, that wove its way through Turkey, Iran, Afghanistan, Pakistan and India.

The fresh and exciting designs of *IT* and *OZ* magazines, with their Alphonse Mucha-inspired graphics, progressive layouts and psychedelic spreads by prominent artists like Martin Sharp, broke every rule in the book, and were largely responsible for spreading the cultural message. They were also vital in promoting events such as the '14 Hour Technicolor Dream' at Alexandra Palace, London, where 41 bands played to an audience of 10,000; the Festival of the Flower Children at Woburn Abbey; and new clubs like Middle Earth.

But one of the greatest events to happen that year was the arrival of Jimi Hendrix. Not only did he bring with him his unique brand of amazing music, but also a fantastically eclectic dress sense that would inspire a mass of new followers.

Left: Fig 1. Black, green and red tie-dye organza fringe top, Germinal Rangel, late 1960s, England. Red crushed velvet dress, late 1960s, England. Silver necklace with bells, mid 1960s, Morocco. Wooden beads necklace.

Fig 2. Cream silk brocade kimono, with gold-work snake decoration, Chinese. Pink polyester tie front shirt, Alkasura, mid 1960s, London. Red and cream tie-dye velvet trousers, mid 1960s, England. Pink paisley silk sash.

Every culture and gender was plundered to achieve his look, which evolved with each appearance and consisted of Afghan waistcoats, frilly shirts, kaftans, tribal jewellery, feathered floppy hats, silk scarves, feather boas, velvet pants and Spanish boots.

I was lucky enough to see him perform at a Leicester University gig with a group of friends that year. Not even knowing who he was, we just happened to be passing the hall and were drawn in by the incredible sounds that were coming out!

Suddenly it seemed as if everyone who became involved with the movement was turned on. Psychedelic music filled the air; kids everywhere cast off their dismal old clothes and wore coats of many colours. Indian jewellery, beads and bells were in abundance, Henna was applied to hair and decorated with flowers, heavy kohl make-up became popular and body painting reached an all-time high. Countless thousands revelled in the powerful messages of peace, and 'make love, not war'. But some members of the general public felt threatened by the Hippie lifestyle and hated their free-thinking ideals; nicknaming them the 'longhairs', many thought they were mad, dirty, irresponsible and generally unacceptable in modern society.

In February 1968, the Beatles gathered together a troop of disciples, and went to India to receive instruction from the Maharishi Mahesh Yogi. Here they found spiritualism and a many-faceted philosophy that included yoga, transcendental meditation and vegetarianism. Spiritualism became a guiding light for an alternative lifestyle, and fitted perfectly the flower children's new way of thinking.

By this time a network of underground and free press, such as *OZ* and *IT* in London, *East Village Other* in NYC, *Suck* in Amsterdam, *Actuel* in Paris and *The Fifth Estate* in Detroit, started by activist and so-called king of the Hippies John Sinclair, were busy spreading the word around the world.

This was also a year of mass student demonstrations, protests and riots, which flared up around the world and raised such issues as opposition to the Vietnam War, racism and civil liberties. The police regularly used clubs against demonstrators, and many arrests were made; during February 1968, in South Carolina, three students died during a demonstration. In April that same year, Martin Luther King Jr was killed, sparking riots all over America, and in October police and troops in Mexico turned their guns on rioting students, killing over 100 people. The gentle Hippies were now in fear of their lives, and in Detroit at least one group armed themselves in self-defence against police brutality and constant harassment.

'The dream of every society is total control'
– Gore Vidal.

Helter Skelter

By 1969, the movement had risen to its peak, with massive numbers of people throughout the world finally waking up to its passive power. This awakening was prompted by several important happenings during the year, which would later go down in the history books as major events in Hippie culture.

In March, John Lennon and Yoko Ono married and started a series of peaceful 'Bed-Ins' as a protest against the Vietnam War. In July, the hugely influential movie *Easy Rider*, directed by Dennis Hopper, who starred along with Peter Fonda and Jack Nicholson, was released. Its poignant storyline drove home how much Hippies were hated by small-town American communities.

Also by this time, in many remote parts of America, deserted ranches and homesteads had been taken over by hundreds of Hippie communes, people who had gone in search of an alternative, shared-resource, back-to-nature lifestyle. However, some of these self-sufficient communes attracted kids who were easily led, and one quasi-commune that sprang up in California was the notorious Manson Family. After initially befriending and working with the Beach Boys' drummer Dennis Wilson on some new tracks, singer-songwriter and guru Charles Manson eventually took over Wilson's home.

Manson began to reveal his evil side, forcing Wilson to have him and his followers physically removed. Manson then relocated to the rundown Spahn Movie Ranch, just outside Los Angeles, where he assembled a feral family of 10 or 12 mainly female followers who, acting on his instructions, murdered actress Sharon Tate and six others over two days in August. Manson claimed he was guided by the lyrics of the Beatles song 'Helter Skelter'.

Right: Fig 1. Cream cheesecloth smock dress with green trim, mid 1960s, India. Silver crucifix on a chain. Tan suede knee length moccasin boots, Minnietonka, Native American Indian. Multi-coloured string scarf.

Fig 5. Brown fringed suede jacket, mid 1960s, London. Brown polyester tie front shirt, Alkasura, mid 1960s, London. Black leather belt with brass buckle, mid 1960s, London. Brown leather trousers, mid 1960s, London. Tan leather strap boots, YSL, mid 1960s Paris.

Fig 6. Sheepskin jacket, late 1960s, England. Black cotton T-shirt with silver Hollywood logo, late 1960s, USA. Bleached blue denim jeans, Falmer, 1960s, England. Tan leather cowboy boots.

Fig 7. Cream and turquoise floral cotton peasant blouse, Aristos, late 1960s, Carnaby Street. Blue denim jeans with paisley inserts, Brutus, 1960s, England. White rope noose. Tan leather cowboy boots.

Left: Dennis Wilson, *Two-Lane Blacktop*, dir Monte Hellman, 1971.

Right: Fig 1. Brown suede fringed Western jacket, mid 1960s, USA. Pink and white tie-dye cheesecloth dress, mid 1960s, India.

Fig 2. Pink cheesecloth dress with embroidered yolk, mid 1960s, India. Wooden bead necklace.

Fig 3. Brown suede beaded waistcoat, mid 1960s, London. Purple embroidered cheesecloth shirt, mid 1960s, India. Green tiered cheesecloth skirt, mid 1960s, India.

Left: Fig 1. Tan suede Western shirt with bone buttons, Lotus, late 1960s, USA. Silver hand pendant on a leather thong. Cream wool T-shirt, late 1960s, England. Blue denim jeans, Wrangler, late 1960s, USA. Tan suede Minnetonka Moccasins, USA.

Fig 2. Black and rust woven cotton Navajo style poncho, USA. Wooden bead necklace. Glass and stone bead necklace. Cream, orange and brown cotton abstract print skirt, late 1960s, England.

Above: Armed Love, Hill Street House, Detroit, 1969, ©Leni Sinclair.

Above: Dennis Hopper, director and co-star, *Easy Rider*, 1969.

Right: Fig 1. Brown suede fur trimmed gilet, late 1960s, England. Blue and pink striped knitted wool dress, late 1960s, England. Amber glass beads.

Fig 2. Olive green cotton army shirt with patches and badges, late 1960s, England. Pink embroidered cotton shirt, late 1960s, India. Blue denim jeans, late 1960s, England. Tan suede espadrilles.

The world and Hippie communities were rocked by the Tate murders, but nonetheless, just one week later, an unprecedented 400,000 fans turned up to watch 32 bands over a long weekend at the Woodstock Festival.

In December, John and Yoko sent a message of peace around the world displayed on huge billboards. The message read: *'WAR IS OVER! If You Want It – Happy Christmas From John and Yoko'.*

By the winter of 1969, even true devotees believed that Hippie culture was becoming far too acceptable to the general public. The clothes that had once seemed so anti-establishment had now become mainstream. Older, straight people began taking on the general Hippie style of dress and liberal attitude towards drug use. In 1973, as America announced that it was pulling out of Vietnam, the movement had already begun to drift apart, with nothing left to protest about.

Although there had been many drug casualties along the way, there was no disputing that the beautiful revolution, for which they had peacefully fought, had happened, and in a big way. But the music, love, drugs, fashion, protest and free expression that had given the Hippie movement its impetus were ultimately not enough to keep it going and, for most, the journey was over.

Left: Anita Pallenberg and Marianne Faithfull, Stones in the Park concert, London, 1969.

Left: Fig 1. Wine velvet tunic top with gold braid, mid 1960s, India. Embroidered tote bag, late 1960s, England. Silver bangle. Blue denim jeans with braid decoration, Wild Oats, late 1960s, England. Black leather Chelsea boots, mid 1960s, England.

Left and right: Fig 2. Yellow satin jacket with psychedelic floral applique and stud detail, Nudies, late 1960s, North Hollywood. Black T-shirt with rainbow stripes, mid 1960s, England. Black leather belt with brass buckle. Soft metal necklace, India. Blue denim jeans, Campari, late 1960s, England. Black leather boots, mid 1960s, England.

Left: Fig 1. White polyester shirt with Lone Star pocket patches, De Luxe Sportswear, late 1960s, USA. Black cotton tie front T-shirt, mid 1960s, England. Blue striped cotton trousers, Talamade Garment, late 1960s, England. White canvas plimsolls.

Fig 2. Pale yellow suede fringed trouser suit, Ossie Clark, late 1960s, London. Brown suede knee boots, late 1960s, England.

Right: Fig 1. Brown and cream striped wool blanket jacket, late 1960s, USA. Blue cotton vest with rainbow patch, late 1960s, England. Brown leather belt with brass buckle, late 1960s, England. Brown wool trousers with cream stripes, late 1960s, England. Beige suede lace-up boots, Tony the Shoemaker, late 1960s, England.

Fig 2. Cream goat skin jacket, late 1960s, England. Cream muslin embroidered peasant blouse, late 1960s, England. Multi-coloured patchwork hot-pants, late 1960s, England. Brown suede lace front knee boots, late 1960s, England.

Fig 3. Floral embroidered silk waistcoat, late 1960s, India. Yellow and blue striped wraparound top, Biba, late 1960s, England. Suede looped belt, late 1960s, England. Blue denim jeans with floral patches, Wrangler, late 1960s, England.

Left: Nic Turner (left) of Hawkwind at the Isle of Wight Festival, 1970.

Right: Fig 1. Cream felted cotton gilet, late 1960s, England. Pink three button cotton T-shirt, late 1960s, England. Multi-coloured velvet and cord patchwork trousers, late 1960s, England. Brown suede boots.

Fig 2. White blue and orange knitted American football top, late 1960s, USA. Blue denim dungarees, Ikeda, late 1960s, USA. Brown leather Chelsea boots, late 1960s, England.

9

THE UPSETTERS

SKINHEADS

LATE 1960s – MID 1970s

Harry Parker, social worker: 'You're out of this room, out of this place. You're back into the world.'

Trevor: 'It's your fucking world, mate, not mine. You can stick it up your arse I don't want it!'

Made in Britain, dir Alan Clarke, 1982.

The roots of Skinhead style and attitude can be traced back to at least 1964, when gangs of aggressive young scooter Mods took to the seaside beaches of Brighton, Margate and Southend in southern England on bank holidays and turned them into battlefields. They caused havoc, coming up against hordes of Rockers and bikers, to whom they took an intense dislike, as well as any members of the general public who happened to be in the way. These early riots would become legendary in scooter Mod folklore, and passed down from generation to generation. They could also be seen as a dress rehearsal for the much-publicised battles caused by marauding gangs of Skinheads that took place on football terraces and adjoining streets during the late 1960s.

Thanks largely to its notoriety in the press, the Mod movement had attracted a massive following by 1966, but most of the movement's originators, who had never been involved in the violence, had moved on to become either new-style Regency dandies or Hippies or – disillusioned by the whole thing, got out of the style race altogether. Hard-to-find clothes that had once been imported or even tailor-made, and that had been saved up for and cherished, were now being copied cheaply and made available in every fashionable shop in every town. Even their beloved soul music and Tamla Motown, which previously could only be heard in exclusive clubs or, occasionally, on pirate radio stations, had gone mainstream, now appearing on the radio and even in the Top 10 charts. Nothing of the old-school scene was now sacred or remotely cool.

Although most Mods were from working-class backgrounds and had decent-paying jobs and good disposable income, between 1964 and 1966 the accent had shifted dramatically from a genuine Mod's ethos of spending all their money buying stylish clothes, dancing to great music and buying a few pep pills, a coffee or a Coke, to these young lookalikes or wannabes were now more interested in drinking alcohol, having a bad attitude and actively looking for trouble. The seaside riots had attracted a much tougher type of kids with a gang mentality, who became known as 'hard Mods'. There was no way these kids would ever become poncey, pretentious dandies or long-haired, smelly Hippies; in fact, moving on from brawls with Rockers, the aforementioned Hippies would become the next in line for these kids to pick on. These so-called hard Mods were arguably the founding fathers of the early Skinhead movement, and some were even their older brothers, whose bragging rights must have influenced many a Skinhead-in-waiting.

Ben Sherman

By the second half of the decade, it was cheaper and easier than ever for any young kid to copy the basic Mod style of cropped hair, a polo shirt, Levi's, desert boots, a parka and a scooter. Indeed any aforementioned item would give the wearer the right to call themselves a Mod. The look by that time had been pared down and was becoming more of a uniform, an aggressive alternative to the peace-and-love brigade in their flowered kaftans and flowing robes.

American Ivy-League-style button-down collar shirts in Oxford cotton had been coveted by Mods since the early 1960s, but they were only available in a few specialist shops as they had to be imported. However, in 1963, in response to a growing demand, a Brighton clothes manufacturer named Arthur Benjamin Sugarman, who had lived for some time in America, started a company called Ben Sherman to produce a good English version of the button-down shirts, which became very popular with younger Mods as they were much cheaper than the original imports.

And by the mid 1960s, most men's stores sold an English fashion version of the shirt. Then in 1966, along came two teenage brothers, named Keith and Alan Freedman, who started a company called Brutus Jeans, supposedly named after the then-popular man's aftershave Brut. The brothers developed a new range of shirt designs called the Brutus Trimfit. Within just a couple of years, they became a huge hit, and went on to be an essential label in all Skinheads' wardrobes. The new shirts were based on the American style that companies such as Brooks Brothers and Arrow manufactured, but were slim-fitting and came in a range of bright-coloured checks and loud plaids. They had a deep, button-down roll collar, and on the back of the shirt there was a button on the collar, a centre pleat and hanger between the shoulders. The short-sleeved version really took off with Skinheads and, of course, again, it was cheaper to buy than the American original.

Wash-and-wear suits had been popular with American businessmen since the 1950s, and the menswear industry was keen to develop new fabrics that would retain their shape. In 1964, the American jean company Levi Strauss & Co announced a new kind of fabric called Levi's Sta-Prest that allowed casual trousers to have permanent creases. These high-waist, flat-front, straight-leg slacks were an instant success and it wasn't long before the Lee Jeans company also produced permanent press trousers. Both versions were very popular with Mods – for not only was this the first truly modern easy care trouser it also was a great shape and style and came in a subtle range of colours that complemented the Mod colour palette. Sta-Prest remained in menswear shops and outfitters throughout the 1960s, and would become much sought after by young Skinheads towards the end of the decade.

Previous page: Tim Roth, *Made In Britain*, dir Alan Clarke, 1982.

Left: Fig 1. Blue denim jacket, Levi's, late 1960s, USA. White cotton T-shirt. Black clip-on braces, late 1960s, England. Blue denim jeans, Levi's 501, USA. Black leather 14-eyelet boots, Dr. Martens, England. Blue and white striped wool football supporter's scarf.

Fig 2. Navy wool and PVC donkey jacket, late 1960s, England. Fine striped cotton union shirt, 1950s, England. White cotton clip-on braces, late 1960s, England. Blue denim jeans, Levi's 501, USA. Black leather 7 eyelet industrial boots, Dr. Martens, England. Blue and white striped wool football supporter's scarf.

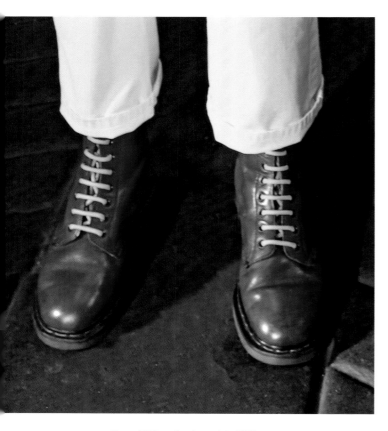

Above: White cotton jeans, late 1960s, England. Cherry red eight-eyelet boots, Dr. Martens, England.

Right: Fig 1. White poly-cotton raincoat, Aquaron 100 by Gleneagles, late 1960s, England. Blue denim jeans, Levi's 501, USA. Cherry red leather eight-eyelet boots, Dr. Martens, England. Red and white striped wool football supporter's scarf.

Fig 2. Olive wool army battledress jacket, 1940s, England. Brown wool trousers, 1960s, England. Black steel toe-cap boots, Dr. Martens, England. Red and white striped wool football supporter's scarf.

Dr. Martens AirWair boots, or DMs, with their famously comfortable bouncing soles, were invented in the late 1940s by a German doctor called Klaus Märtens, but it was not until 1960 that they came to England, worn chiefly at that time by factory workers and postmen who were on their feet all day. These were not your normal, everyday, cheap ex-army-style work boots, such as those worn by builders or coal miners; Dr. Martens were lighter and softer with more flexible leather, and quite expensive by comparison. Skinheads were the first youth sub-culture to pick up on the boots' stylish quality and comfort, and they quickly adopted both the cherry-red and black versions as an important part of their own uniform. Fred Perry three-button polo shirts that had been a Mod staple now also became an essential part of the Skinhead style.

By 1968, the Skinhead look as we know it – No. 2 cropped hair and shaved-in parting, button-down collar shirt, Levi's Sta-Prest or ankle-swinging 501 jeans, DMs, skinny braces and a sheepskin coat – was starting to come together, worn by young, working-class lads on football terraces across Britain.

According to Jim Ferguson's amazingly detailed fashion notebook in the seminal 1982 book *Skinhead* by Nick Knight, *'A sheepskin was the skinhead status symbol. From the kick-off in '68 to the final whistle in '71 the coat could be worn with pride.'* He goes on, *'At the start – '68, '69, any shirt that was not "fashion" was worn – old men's collarless & collared baggy-bodied styles, T-shirts, etc. Some early skinheads went awry & wore tie-dyed granddad vests.'*

I can remember one Saturday afternoon, probably in the winter of 1969, passing the entrance of the main rail station in my home town of Leicester, and seeing hordes of young kids with very cropped hair for the first time, all wearing Ben Sherman button-down style shirts, slim braces on their short jeans, highly polished red Doc Marten boots, and striped football supporter's scarves, either tied around their necks like a cravat, or wrists in a display of fearless bravado. It was the same picture in town centres up and down the country.

The Skinhead look would become an increasingly familiar sight as numbers grew over the next few years, but at the time it was quite rare to see a shaved head, particularly as most young men (and even TV news presenters) had either long hair or a beard, or both, and wore flared jeans, so this style really stood out.

The severe paramilitary look and stance that Skinheads adopted could also have been inspired by the buzz-cut hair and high-leg boots of the US Marines, who at the time were fighting in the Vietnam War, so regularly featured on TV news programmes.

Above: Skinheads, London, 1970.

Right: Brown sheepskin coat, late 1960s, England. Green striped Oxford cotton button-down shirt, Airman Traditionals, late 1960s, England. Red clip-on braces, late 1960s, England. White cotton jeans, late 1960s, England. Red and white striped wool football supporter's scarf.

Above: Skinheads and hippies, Trafalgar Square, London, 1969.

Right: Fig 1. Beige cotton cardigan with orange trim, Harry Fenton, late 1960s, Shaftsbury Avenue, London. Orange and yellow check button-down collar shirt, Arrow TTM, late 1960s, USA. White clip-on braces, late 1960s, England. Blue denim jeans, Levi's 501, USA. Cherry red eight-eyelet boots, Dr. Martens.

Fig 2. Orange and green check cotton button-down collar shirt, John Wells, late 1960s, England. Red clip-on braces, late 1960s, England. Beige cotton jeans, Levi's 501, USA. Cherry red eight-eyelet boots, Dr. Martens, England.

Left: Fig 1. Beige cotton cardigan with orange trim, Harry Fenton, late 1960s, Shaftsbury Avenue, London. Orange and yellow check button-down collar shirt, Arrow TTM, late 1960s, USA. White clip-on braces, late 1960s, England. Blue denim jeans, Levi's 501, USA. Cherry red eight-eyelet boots, Dr. Martens.

Fig 2. Cream cotton polo shirt, Fred Perry, late 1960s, England. Black clip-on braces, late 1960s, England. Yellow perma-press trousers, Campari, late 1960s, England. Cherry red eight-eyelet boots, Dr. Martens, England.

Fig 3. Brown wool cardigan, Browns, late 1960s, England. Yellow check cotton button-down collar shirt, Campus Ivy Traditionals, late 1960s, USA. Maroon clip-on braces, late 1960s, England. Blue denim bleached jeans, Levi's 501, USA. Red cotton socks. Black leather 14-eyelet boots, Dr. Martens, England.

Right: Skinheads, Coventry, 1969.

Yell

Once they had become recognised as a full-scale movement through their antics at football matches, Skinheads were always in the press and they became known as 'boot boys' or 'Peanuts' for obvious reasons. Some hard cases actually wore steel toecap work boots and these became banned at matches after serious damage was caused by the wearers in fights with supporters from opposing teams who, incidentally, could now only be told apart by the scarf colours they flew.

Over the next couple of years, the numbers of Skinheads turning up at matches grew into thousands, like small armies. They posed a genuine threat to the safety of the public and each other, so much so that before a match the police would line the kids up and remove, or even cut, the laces of their boots so that they couldn't run away from trouble after a match. Testosterone-laden, these kids loved to fight, and particularly revelled in racist attacks. And if there was no one around to intimidate, they would fight among themselves, in a constant challenge to their own pack leaders.

As with most of the sub-cultures mentioned in this book, there was a great sense of camaraderie among the Skinheads, mainly due to their background and football-team fanaticism, not to mention strength in numbers. Although much has been made of Skinheads hating Hippies and beating them up just because of the way they looked, in fact, from 1969 the influential Hippie newspaper *IT* (*International Times*), actually ran a regular column called 'Yell', which was about Skinheads, for Skinheads, written by Skinheads. Perhaps inviting them into the fold was a Hippie ploy to try to create a harmonious fear-free society that we could all live in together.

The other great love and driving force of the early Skinheads was music: they listened to ska, Bluebeat, rocksteady and even soul music early on, which they also inherited from Mods, and they would later claim reggae as their own true music (anything from the Trojan record label, formed in 1968, would have credibility). Artists such as Desmond Dekker, Prince Buster, the Skatellites and the Upsetters were guaranteed to fill the dance floor. A lot of the music and Skinhead style can also be attributed to Jamaican Rude Boys who were a great influence. Early on in their career even the Wolverhampton band Slade wore the Skinhead look.

Left: Fig 1. Black cotton Harrington jacket, 1970s, England. White cotton polo shirt, Fred Perry, 1970s, England. Black cotton skirt, late 1960s, England. White lace tights. Black leather eight-eyelet boots, Dr. Martens, England.

Fig 2. Black cotton Harrington jacket, 1970s, England. White nylon polo shirt, late 1960s, England. White trousers, Sta-Prest, 1970s, England. Black leather boxing boots, 1970s, England.

Right: Fig 1. Navy wool Crombie style overcoat, England. Navy and white check button-down shirt, 1970s, England. White pocket hanky held with pearl tie tack. Blue denim jeans, Levi's 501, USA. Black leather 14-eyelet boots, Dr. Martens, England.

Fig 2. Navy wool Crombie style overcoat, 1970s, England. Red cotton plaid shirt, Darwin, 1970s, USA. Red silk hanky held with red stone tie-tack. Buff denim jeans, 1970s, England. Black leather eight-eyelet boots, Dr. Martens, England.

Above: Suedeheads, London, 1971.

Right: Fig 1. Beige mohair jacket, Hardy Amies by Hepworth, late 1960s, England. Maroon silk hanky held by maroon glass tie-tack. Fine check button-down collar shirt, Brooks Brothers, USA. Black mohair trousers, late 1960s, England. Red cotton socks. Oxblood tassle loafers, Loakes, England.

Fig 2. Teal shot with red tonic jacket, early 1970s, England. Fine check shirt, Wemblex, early 1970s, England. Pale blue hanky held by blue glass stone tie-tack. Black mini-skirt, early 1970s, England. Green leather Mary Jane style shoes, Anello & Davide, early 1970s, England.

Fig 3. Deep red shot with black tonic jacket, early 1970s, England. Red silk hanky held by red glass stone tie-tack. Pink cotton button-down shirt, Ben Sherman, early 1970s, England. Black velvet skirt, early 1970s, England. Oxblood penny loafers, Bass Weejun, early 1970s, USA.

Fig 4. Grey shot with green tonic suit, John Collier, early 1970s, England. Red silk hanky held by red glass stone tie-tack. Yellow Oxford cotton button-down shirt, Arrow, early 1970s, USA. Maroon cotton socks. Black leather brogues, early 1970s, England.

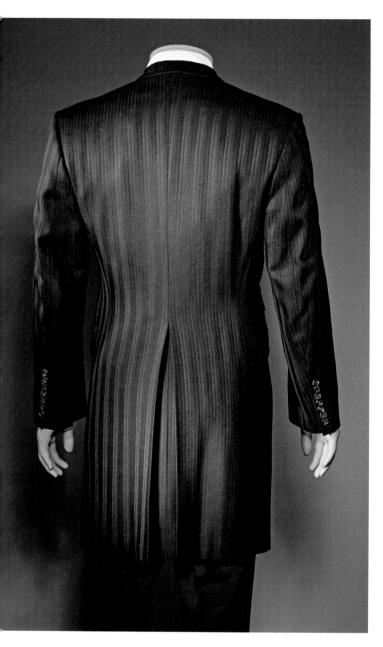

Above and right: Fig 1. Blue and bronze striped worsted frock coat, Henry London, Clapham Junction, early 1970s, England. Striped button-down shirt, Brooks Brothers, early 1970s, USA. Brown pocket hanky held by blue glass stone tie-tack. Navy mohair trousers, early 1970s, England. Black cotton socks. Black leather brogue shoes, Lloyd, early 1970s, Germany.

Fig 2. Black velvet mini-dress with silk tartan details, early 1970s, England. Black patent granny shoes with side buckle, Camalots QualiCraft, mid 1960s, USA.

At the Skinhead movement's height in 1970, a small publishing company called New English Library reacted to a series of dramatic press headlines about Skinhead forays, formulating an idea to produce a series of sub-culture pulp fiction books that would capitalise on the growing phenomenon. This started in 1970 with *Skinhead*, written by Richard Allen, about the exploits of one Joe Hawkins. His life and daily experiences many readers believed were so realistic and lifelike, they could only have been written by a genuine Skinhead.

The book was immensely successful and actually turned the company's fortunes around. Allen would go on to write a further 17 novels for the company that covered Mods, Punks and Glam, but they were mostly about Skinheads.

In 1996, the BBC put out a fascinating documentary called *Skinhead Farewell* about the life of Richard Allen, whose real name turned out to be James Moffat, a Canadian author living in England and who at the time of writing *Skinhead* was actually 55 years old. During his life he wrote around 290 novels under at least 45 different pseudonyms.

A British comedy movie entitled *The Breaking of Bumbo*, 1970, directed by Andrew Sinclair, has some really great riot footage of early Skinheads wearing period-correct outfits.

In all violence-based youth cults, it is always the lads who make the newspaper headlines and get all the attention but, of course, behind the scenes, the Skinhead girl movement was just as big and supportive. Most wore variations of the fashion of the day, again pretty similar to Mod girls, such as simple round neck sweaters, mini-skirts, lace tights and clumpy shoes, and some dressed just like the boys in button downs, braces, jeans and Dr. Martens. And again the one thing that really made them stand out was their short, cropped, boyish haircuts – this look, too, had come directly from the unisex cuts the Mods had earlier established. One of the most popular and copied haircuts for Skinhead girls was the feather cut. The beautiful soul singer Julie Driscoll, who had great short hair early on as a Mod, was a huge influence here, and most Skinhead girls copied her false eyelashes, smudged make-up and hairstyle when she adopted the feather cut in 1969.

But by 1970, boy's haircuts that only a year before had got down to a No. 1 clip cut were being grown out, and this slightly longer hairstyle started to be referred to as Suedehead. Along with a new haircut came a fresh smart casual look, which now required a polo-, round- or V-neck sweater and shirt to be worn with either jeans or Sta-Prest trousers, and loafers or wing-tip brogues. Suits were also an important part of this move to a more formal-looking profile. That same year there was a great photo shoot in *Mirabelle* magazine titled 'Skinheads in Focus', of kids wearing the style.

Keep the Faith

During the early days of the Mod movement, in 1957, the French textile company Dormeuil developed a new three-ply mohair-and-wool-mix suiting called Tonik, which retained the deep lustrous quality and sheen of mohair. Blended with the right colours, Tonik had a wonderful two-tone iridescent effect that Mods loved but like mohair it was very expensive. By the time Suedeheads had picked up on the qualities and unique look of the fabric, Tonik (or 'tonic') had become the generic name for any two-tone suiting and many cheaper copies had been developed by other textile manufactures; a Tonik suit became the must-have addition to both Suedehead boys' and girls' wardrobes. The fabric came in the wildest combinations of colours, but most popular were fawn shot with green, purple shot with green and maroon shot with black or blue.

The style of suit once again took inspiration from the Mods; high-fastening narrow lapels, single breasted with three- or four-buttons, deep sloping pocket flaps, at least one (and sometimes multiple) ticket pockets, a really long centre vent, and multiple buttons on the cuffs. Girls' suits, too, would sometimes have extreme detail just like the boys'. Also popular were raised seams and hand-picked stitching on the lapels. Crombie-style coats in either navy or black really came into their own, as did Harrington jackets, and by 1971 the look was becoming much more smart casual, with many kids influenced by the new TV series *Budgie*, starring Adam Faith, who wore longer hair and fashion shirts with long beagle ear collars, teamed with bold check trousers. The show was so popular it even had a bomber jacket named after it, aptly called a 'Budgie jacket', and all the kids wore them. A nice little article called 'Meet the Crombie Boys' appeared in *The Sunday Times Magazine* in March 1971 that showed both boys and girls wearing the Suedehead style.

This was the same year that the controversial movie *A Clockwork Orange*, directed by Stanley Kubrick, was released. Based on a 1962 novel by Anthony Burgess, the story is set in the near future and depicts the antics of an extremely violent gang of youths called Droogs. Much has been made over the years about the similarity of the characters in the film and the Skinheads.

By 1972, the Skinhead and Suedehead music scene and look was beginning to lose its popularity, and kids were on the lookout for something else. Many found a new direction and drive from the nascent Northern Soul scene, where at the weekends, kids from northern mill towns, who also followed football, obsessed over dancing. Their big thing was collecting rare, high-energy, fast-tempo soul music records from the mid 1960s, which would be bought and played at amphetamine-fuelled all-nighters.

Because of the extremely energetic and elaborate nature of the dances, most boys and girls took to wearing athletic vests and very high-waisted, extremely wide leg baggy trousers called Spencers, which like their early predecessors, Oxford bags, were very popular with undergraduates during the 1920s.

By the mid 1970s, just as Punk was emerging in London, sportswear worn as casual clothing was becoming more and more popular, particularly among Northern Soul devotees and legions of football fans. Designer-labelled warm-up jackets and early trainers by Adidas worn with baggies or wide, flared jeans formed the basis of the Scally and early Casual look that would dominate the football terraces during the later end of the decade and through into the 1980s, when, ironically, there was a full scale Skinhead revival.

In 1983 a graphic play called *Made in Britain*, directed by Alan Clarke, was shown on British TV. The play looked in depth at the life and times of a violent 16-year-old anti-authoritarian, racist Skinhead brilliantly played by Tim Roth.

Left: Fig 1. Ginger and green herringbone worsted tailored suit, John Collier, early 1970s, England. Navy wool knit shirt, California Gold, early 1970s, USA. Red silk pocket handkerchief. Red cotton socks. Black leather loafers.

Fig 2. Black, red and yellow striped jersey mini-dress, Bobi Bartlett, early 1970s, England. Black leather loafers, Faith, 1970s, London.

Fig 3. White and brown diamond pattern acrylic tank top, Harold Ingram, 1970s, England. Beige cotton dog ear collar shirt, early 1970s, England. Burgundy velvet mini-skirt, 1970s, England. White cotton knee socks. Cream patent tassel loafers, T Elliott & Sons, 1970s, London.

Above: 'Jook', 1973, ©Gered Mankowitz.

Right: Fig 1. White toweling vest, Adidas, 1970s, England. Yellow cotton paisley scarf. Duck egg blue gabardine trousers, 1970s, England. Duck egg blue suede lace-up shoes, 1970s, England.

Fig 2. Tan leather jacket, 1970s, England. Peach vest top, 1970s, England. Brown woven leather belt. Brown gabardine trousers, 1970s, England. Brown and cream leather loafers, 1970s, England.

Above: Fig 1. Blue denim jeans, Wrangler, 1970s, USA. White canvas boxing boots, Coasters, 1970s, England.

Fig 2. Black gabardine trousers, 1970s, England. Brown leather slip-on shoes, with tassel detail, Moreschi, 1970s, Italy.

Right: Fig 1. Red and white nylon blouson jacket, 1970s, England. Blue denim skirt, 1970s, England. White cotton socks. Red and white canvas shoes, Converse, USA.

Fig 2. Grey, maroon and white striped T-shirt, Adidas, 1970s, England. Grey leather belt, 1970s, England. Ginger gabardine baggies, Johnson & Johnson, 1970s, London. Oxblood leather brogues, Ikon Originals, 1970s style, England.

Fig 3. Red cotton sports top, 1970s, England. White vinyl belt. Grey flannel culottes, 1970s, England. White cotton socks. Black leather shoes, K Skips, 1970s, England.

Left: Fig 1. Maroon and grey polyester warm-up jacket, Admiral, 1970s, England. Navy cord jeans, Levis, 1970s, USA. Maroon leather bowling shoes, 1970s, England.

Fig 2. Green and white striped acrylic cardigan, 1970s, England. White, green and red seersucker check dog ear shirt, Jaytex, 1970s, London. Blue denim jeans, Wrangler, 1970s, USA. White canvas boxing boots, Coasters, 1970s, England.

Fig 3. Black and Shetland wool sweater with white argyle yolk, Glenair, 1970s, Edinburgh. Cream cotton dog ear collar shirt, Rox, 1970s, England. Black gabardine trousers, 1970s, England. Brown leather slip-on shoes, with tassel detail, Moreschi, 1970s, Italy.

Fig 4. Navy and white houndstooth pattern wool sweater, 1970s, England. Grey multi-pleat baggies, Spencers, 1970s, England. Red leather shoes, K Shoes, 1970s, England.

10

DISOBEY

PUNKS

MID – LATE 1970s

"In those days, desires weren't allowed to become reality. So fantasy was substituted for them – films, books, pictures. They called it 'art'. But when your desires become reality, you don't need fantasy any longer, or art."

Amyl Nitrite, *Jubilee*, Derek Jarman, 1977.

The first seeds of the British Punk movement began to germinate in 1971, when Malcolm McLaren and his partner Vivienne Westwood set up a small operation selling 1950s and 1960s rock 'n' roll records, objects and ephemera from the back room of Paradise Garage, a trendy vintage American denim shop at 430 Kings Road, World's End, Chelsea.

Tired of Hippie complacency, the couple were inspired by a recent rock 'n' roll revival, and within a few months they had taken over the running of the shop, completely redecorated the interior to resemble a Modernist 1950s living room, and renamed it Let It Rock. The walls, displays and racks were now filled with original and retro-designed Teddy Boy and Teddy Girl clothes, records, guitar-shaped mirrors and rock 'n' roll posters and photos. An early flyer proclaimed 'Teddy Boys forever! The Rock-era is our business'. It did not take long before hordes of Teddy Boy revivalists found the shop, attracted by the interior's authentic ambience, its stock of rare 1950s clothes and made-to-measure drapes.

The shop's black-painted exterior and large fluorescent-pink painted letters stood out like a sore thumb on the Kings Road, especially as World's End was still very much a Hippie heartland, with shops like Gandalf's Garden, The Sweet Shop and others that stocked kaftans, robes, incense and other eastern delights; just a few doors away was the infamous Granny Takes a Trip. Granny's, renowned for its dramatic, pop art shop fronts, had been the number one stop for Hippie royalty since it opened in 1965. But by 1971 the shops had new owners, who focused more on supplying glittery, embellished, Western-influenced suits and stage clothes to music celebrities such as Marc Bolan, Gram Parsons and Keith Richards.

Saturdays were the big day at Let it Rock, and McLaren would sometimes spend all of the night before and most of Saturday morning preparing displays of the clothes,

much to the frustration of the shop's customers who
queued for hours to get in. It did not take long for the
shop to become a victim of its own success, and with
that McLaren became less tolerant of the Teds' purist
approach towards the clothes. The shop had become
a hangout, and some customers would spend hours
discussing whether or not the stock of florescent socks
were the correct shade of green or pink that they were
in the 1950s. He felt this train-spotter attitude was
stifling the couple's growing creativity, which by then
was developing into a rebellious free spirit.

In 1973, the couple transformed the shop again into
Too Fast To Live, Too Young To Die. Now stocked with
a much tougher, fetishist Rocker style of clothing,
the revamped shop with its new name drew in a more
adventurous type of customer looking for American
zoot suits, original 1950s fleck jackets, peg-top trousers,
old leather biker jackets, studded leather miniskirts,
customised mohair tops and stiletto shoes.

They also began to experiment with basic printing
and dyeing techniques on capped sleeve T-shirts,
to which they added chains, studs and crude appliqué,
and although very labour-intensive, this fresh approach
and custom DIY look to the clothes, with its primitive
tribal influences, would later become one of their
established trademarks.

Later that year, as a way of promoting the shop,
McLaren and Westwood attended a trade fair in New York
that they remembered as a complete disaster, as no one
understood the retro 1950s look they were trying to sell.
But they were introduced to the New York Dolls, a band
who were dressed in trashy drag, like cheap transvestites
with their backcombed hair, outrageous make-up,
skin-tight clothes and high-heeled shoes.

The Dolls played a rough-and-ready style of rock 'n'
roll that was clearly influenced by earlier proto-Punk
bands such as MC5, the Velvet Underground and the
Stooges. McLaren was immediately drawn to the band's
look and audacious attitude; he thought the fact that they
couldn't actually sing or play guitars that well was a bonus.
Being so intrigued, in 1975, he actually ended up managing
them for a few months, just before they broke up.

During this time, he dressed them in outlandish red
Ciré, vinyl and patent leather costumes and designed
a stylised version of the hammer and sickle logo to
promote them. He had already begun to nurture the
idea that clothing could be used as a vehicle to deliver
messages of political subversion, to confront and
provoke the establishment, so with this look he really
hoped the band would appear to be communist
sympathisers and therefore upset the American public.

Left: Fig 1. String hangman's sweater, Seditionaries, mid 1970s, London. Oliver Twist print T-shirt, Seditionaries, late 1970s, London. Black cotton bondage trousers, Seditionaries, mid 1970s, London. Tan and green strap and buckle boots, Seditionaries, late 1970s, London.

Fig 2. S&M studded leather harness, mid 1970s, England.

Fig 3. Mohair sweater, Seditionaries, mid 1970s, London. Black leather skirt, mid 1970s, England. White leather pointed stiletto shoes, 1970s, England.

Fig 4. Pink cotton and chicken bones T-shirt remade by Joe Corré, Let it Rock, 1990s, London. Black leather belt, 1970s, England. White net petticoat, 1970s, England. Black leather bikini bottoms, Sex Original, 1970s, London. White patent court shoes, Let it Rock, early 1970s, London. Pearl necklace.

Fig 5. Black studded Dominator T-shirt remade by Joe Corré, Let it Rock, 1990s, London. Red cotton jeans, Smiths, mid 1970s, USA.

Left: Pink cotton and chicken bones T-shirt remade by Joe Corré, Let it Rock, 1990s, London. Black leather belt, 1970s, England. White net petticoat, 1970s, England. Black leather bikini bottoms, Sex Original, 1970s, London. Pearl necklace.

Right: 1. 1950s style grey leather shoes, Let It Rock, early 1970s.

2. Mohair sweater, Seditionaries, mid 1970s, London. Black leather skirt, mid 1970s, England.

Left: Green and red striped mohair sweater, Seditionaries, mid 1970s, London. Khaki cotton trousers, Sex Original, mid 1970s, England.

Right: Fig 1. White Rayon 1950s fleck shirt, Measuremade, 1970s, England. Roxy club owner Andrew Czezowski was inadvertently stabbed with a pair of scissors by Sid Vicious in this shirt as he tried to separate a fight between Ari Up and Sid. White Sid Vicious Destroy print T-shirt, late 1970s, England. Royal blue gabardine peg top trousers, Acme Attractions, mid 1970s, London. Red plastic jelly sandals, Sarrai Lienne, mid 1970s, France.

Fig 2. Green and red striped mohair sweater, Seditionaries, mid 1970s, London. Black studded leather choker, 1970s, England. Khaki cotton trousers, Sex Original, mid 1970s, England. Brown plastic sandals, Plastishus, mid 1970s, England.

"Ello Joe, Been anywhere lately
Nah, its all played aht Bill,
Gettin to straight."

For some time, the couple had also been fascinated with the imagery of underground sexual culture – bondage, fetishism, sado-masochism and pornography – and while McLaren had been promoting the Dolls in New York, Westwood had been busy designing a series of sexually explicit T-shirts. One of her assistants was actually arrested in Trafalgar Square for wearing a T-shirt design that featured two half-naked cowboys with their penises almost touching; he was charged and fined with indecency. There followed a vice squad raid on the shop with the police confiscating all the offending T-shirts. McLaren and Westwood eventually ended up in court and were fined on the grounds of indecent exhibition, but this charge only fuelled their contempt for censorship and authority even more.

So shortly afterwards, in 1974, as an act of direct confrontation and defiance, they changed the name of the shop to SEX, and now three huge pink vinyl letters dominated its frontage, assaulting passers-by with their powerful graphics, behind which they had hand-scrawled, *'Craft must have clothes but Truth loves to go naked'*.

The shop's highly provocative T-shirt prints, fetishist rubber and leatherwear became the subject of growing interest, not only to fashionable kids but also to the vice squad, and again several arrests were made on the grounds of obscenity.

Fired up by his involvement with the New York Dolls, McLaren started to realise the potential of creating a home-grown anarchic band that he could cultivate and fully exploit in England and, as he put it, *'give the clothes a voice'*. He had to look no further than the shop itself to find some budding musicians, and in 1975 the Sex Pistols were born.

With each successive shop, McLaren and Westwood's radical clothing designs increasingly challenged the conventions of their growing clientele, while clearly steering them into the direction of forming a new, quite revolutionary youth movement. Moving on rapidly from the earlier glorification of pure nostalgic images of 1950s rock 'n' roll heroes, into an intensely creative phase that was centred around chaos and the destruction of those early roots; sex, raw rock 'n' roll, pop and classical art, political and situationist slogans, death, destruction and degradation all began to appear in their designs.

The shock value and juxtaposition of such diverse influences that went into creating the look became an artistic statement in itself, and this had all the energy, positivity and aggression that was required for a new movement, which McLaren and Westwood later maintained had been their intention from the outset.

Above: Simon Barker of the Bromley Contingent in a Seditionaries Anarchy shirt, Wessex Recording Studios, London, 1976.

Left: Fig 1. Black and white tartan wool zip jacket, mid 1970s, England. White Cowboy print T-shirt, Boy reprint of Seditionaries, 1980s, England. Black bondage trousers, Seditionaries, mid 1970s, London.

Fig 2. Navy wool school blazer mid 1970s, England. Red and black striped mohair sweater, Seditionaries, mid 1970s, London.

Right: Fig 1. White cotton string vest, mid 1970s, England. Black, yellow and red striped school tie, 1970s, England. Red Ciré leggings, mid 1970s, England. Black pointed stiletto buckle front shoes, mid 1970s, England.

Fig 2. Black and tan bleach striped Anarchy shirt, mid 1970s, England. Black vinyl trousers, mid 1970s, England. SS replica armband, Italy. Black leather boots, Dr. Martens, England.

Fig 3. Black and white tartan wool zip jacket, mid 1970s, England. White Cowboy print T-shirt, Boy reprint of Seditionaries, 1980s, England. Black bondage trousers and mini-kilt, Seditionaries, mid 1970s, London. White leather crepe-soled shoes, Fifties Flash, Jack Geach, 1970s, Harrow, England.

Fig 4. Navy wool school blazer decorated with German iron cross medal, handcuff tie clip, and swastika armband, mid 1970s, England. Red and black striped mohair sweater, Seditionaries, mid 1970s, London. Black denim jeans, 1970s, England. Black leather strap bondage boots, Seditionaries, mid 1970s, London.

Above: Kings Road Punks, London, 1977.

Right: Fig 1. Navy wool school blazer with badges, mid 1970s, England. White Generation X T-shirt, Boy, late 1970s, London. Navy cord bondage trousers, Seditionaries, mid 1970s, London. Black suede snow boots, Seditionaries, mid 1970s, London.

Fig 2. Pink mohair sweater, mid 1970s, England. Black fishnet top, mid 1970s, England. Green and gold rayon school tie, 1970s, England. Black wool skirt, 1970s, England. Black leather Monkey boots, 1970s, England.

Fig 3. Grey, blue and red striped school blazer, mid 1970s, England. White cotton graffiti shirt, mid 1970s, England. Red and orange stripe rayon tie, 1970s, England. Black fishnet tights, 1970s, England. Cherry red eight-eyelet boots, Dr. Martens, England.

Fig 4. Brown wool gabardine raincoat with badges and chaos patch, Cravenette, 1950s, England. Brown and pink tie-dye tab collar shirt, Wemblex, 1960s, England. Red and maroon striped tie, 1970s, England. Black leather belt. Black cotton combat trousers, mid 1970s, England. Black leather combat boots, 1970s, England.

For Soldiers, Prostitutes, Dykes and Punks

Fuelled by the success of the Sex Pistols' anarchic performances, during 1976 the Sex shop mutated once again, this time into Seditionaries: Clothes for Heroes. Here, McLaren and Westwood finally unleashed their greatest creation, and Punk in all its glory became a reality. Hidden behind the shop's opaque glass frontage, stood a totally rebuilt interior – part gym, part clinic – with racks of their most innovative and complete collection of designs yet. There featured new unisex paramilitary-style uniforms, parachute shirts, bondage suits, strapped and zipped bondage trousers, muslin T-shirts with colourful subversive prints, multi-strap and spiked crepe-soled boots and army-style berets, all set against a dramatic photographic backdrop of bombed-out Dresden, and an upside down Piccadilly Circus. This was Punk clothing at its most creative and sophisticated.

All of their shops had been designed like theatrical stage sets, emitting a strange elixir of intimidation and attraction that was repellent to those who were unfamiliar while at the same time intoxicating to the regulars – every visit was an experience. For some, just crossing the threshold and actually buying something was an initiation rite in itself, which gave customers a unique sense of belonging to an exclusive club, or cult, whose elitist members shared the same eclectic taste. In this way, the McLaren-Westwood Molotov design cocktail always hit the spot.

Kids wearing elements of Punk-style clothing were first spotted at gigs of bands like the Sex Pistols and the Damned in early 1976, and although Sex and Seditionaries may have been the catalyst for the style, DIY was the order of the day, and pretty soon ripped clothes decorated with safety pins, badges and chains became more common. Other, less intimidating London shops, such as Boy, Smutz and Fifth Column, were quick to open up, selling Punk-style clothing, and all had a keen following. In some ways, they actually had the edge over Seditionaries because their stock of ex-army jackets and trousers, which had been dyed black and had zips, studs, safety pins and rips applied, was a lot cheaper and more accessible.

My partner Rick Carter and I had been supplying all the London vintage and retro shops such as Let it Rock, Acme Attractions, Marx and Johnsons with original period clothes since the early 1970s, and being free agents we were in the perfect position to observe the various shifts in style as they happened, and witness the friendly rivalry between the shops, who on the whole knew each other and got on. However, everyone was always intrigued by what was happening at 430 Kings Road, so rumours were rife. This was partly because you couldn't really see what was going on through the windows; also the shop was continually changing its name and appearance, and these strangely dressed kids would be seen going in and out. It was an incredibly creative time with this fusion of retro and vintage styles, elements of new wave, soul boy and Punk appearing on the streets and in the clubs, all at the same time.

Left: Punks, London, 1977.

Right: 1. Navy cord bondage trousers, Seditionaries, mid 1970s, London. Black suede snow boots, Seditionaries, mid 1970s, London. Black leather Monkey boots, 1970s, England.

2. Grey, blue and red striped school blazer, mid 1970s, England. Brown wool gabardine raincoat with badges and chaos patch, Cravenette.

3. Navy wool school blazer with badges, mid 1970s, England. White Generation X T-shirt, Boy, late 1970s, London.

Right: Fig 1. Black cotton Vive le Rock print T-shirt, Seditionaries, mid 1970s, London. Black cotton bondage trousers, mid 1970s, London. Red leather strap boots, Seditionaries, mid 1970s, London.

Fig 2. Black leather jacket, 1970s, London. Yellow leopard print T-shirt, mid 1970s, London. Black studded leather belt and wristband, mid 1970s, London. Black cotton zip bondage trousers, mid 1970s, London. Black studded leather biker boots, Boy, late 1970s, London.

Fig 3. Black wool cropped jacket, 1970s, London. White cotton God Save the Queen T-shirt, Seditionaries, late 1970s, London. Studded black leather belt, 1970s, London. Black cotton trousers, 1970s, London.

Fig 4. Black leather biker jacket, 1970s, London. Black cotton shirt, 1970s, London. Red Ciré tie, 1960s, London. Black leather belt. Black combat trousers, 1970s, London.

Left: Fig 1. Black cotton Vive le Rock print T-shirt, Seditionaries, mid 1970s, London.

Fig 2. Black leather jacket, 1970s, London. Yellow leopard print T-shirt, mid 1970s, London. Black studded leather belt and wristband, mid 1970s, London. Black cotton zip bondage trousers, mid 1970s, London.

Above left: Black cotton bondage trousers, mid 1970s, London. Red leather strap boots, Seditionaries, mid 1970s, London. Black cotton zip bondage trousers, mid 1970s, London. Black studded leather biker boots, Boy, late 1970s, London.

Above right. Black cotton Vive le Rock print T-shirt, Seditionaries, mid 1970s, London.

Right. Anarchy in the UK Sex Pistols print beret, Seditionaries mid 1970s.

Above: White cotton God Save the Queen
T-shirt, Seditionaries, late 1970s, London.

Right: Fig 1. Black wool cropped
jacket, 1970s, London. White cotton
God Save the Queen T-shirt, Seditionaries,
late 1970s, London. Studded black
leather belt, 1970s, London. Black
cotton trousers, 1970s, London.

Fig 2. Black leather biker jacket, 1970s,
London. Black cotton shirt, 1970s, London.
Red Ciré tie, 1960s, London. Black leather
belt. Black combat trousers, 1970s, London.

Actually Malcolm and I had unwittingly crossed paths
some years before, when we were both buying 1960s
dead stock shirts from an old manufacture in Portsmouth.
As I was selling hundreds of the shirts as pure vintage
examples to eager Japanese buyers, Vivienne and Malcolm
were individually dying, printing and customising the
same items to create their inspired and much copied
Anarchy Shirts.

For a time even Rick and I bought, dyed and sold loads of
ex-army fatigues to Punk shops up and down the country,
but one of our greatest finds was a manufacturer of clear
Perspex wraparound safety glasses whose streamlined
style hadn't changed since their creation in the 1960s.
After much research we located a button dyer who was
prepared to tint the glasses in black, blue, red and green.
Sometimes the dye would react with the Perspex making
them virtually impossible to see through, but it didn't seem
to matter, as every punk worth their salt bought a pair and
we sold thousands right across the UK and Europe.

I remember a group of us going on a clothes-buying
trip to the Paris flea market in late 1977. We all wore
elements of clothes from Seditionaries, and I had on
a God Save the Queen T-shirt. It felt as if we were
committing an act of blasphemy as outraged Parisians
threw us a barrage of abusive remarks and threatening
looks. In the same year filmmaker John Samson put out
a controversial documentary called *Dressing for Pleasure*
about the fetish rubber and leather scene. The film, which
was banned at the time by London Weekend Television,
features both McLaren and Westwood in their shop SEX,
along with muse Jordan.

In 1978 at the height of Punk, Rick and I decided to go
into partnership with old friends Stephane Raynor and
Helen Robinson who had originally been involved with
Acme Attractions and started Boy, to open PX in Covent
Garden. We wanted to take a radically different stance to
the many Punk shops that had sprung up in London and
create a kind of chic fascistic-inspired look, so we stocked
up with black shirts, original German military long black
leather coats, riding breeches and jack boots from the
1940s and 1950s. I designed the shop and refitted the
interior with obsolete industrial units salvaged from the
old MI5 building in Mayfair. The shop received a lot of
press and quickly attracted a discerning fashion crowd.
But my involvement with the project was to be short-lived,
as I was keen to get back on the road again, and sell off
some of the huge stock of vintage clothes I was storing.

In 1978, director Derek Jarman released the film
Jubilee. It was named for Queen Elizabeth II's Silver
Jubilee in 1977 and set against a post-apocalyptic
backdrop with a cast of genuine Punks, such as
Jordan from Seditionaries and pop star Adam Ant.

The film portrays a time in the near future when law and order have broken down and anarchy reigns. It centres on a visitation to this future by Queen Elizabeth I, and three Punk girls who murder people just to relieve the boredom. In an open letter to Derek Jarman, written and printed on a T-shirt of her own design, Vivienne Westwood condemned the film as: 'the most boring and therefore disgusting film I had ever seen'.

A year later, McLaren and Westwood decided to close down Seditionaries, as once again they turned their backs on the monster they had created, and for many of the original Punks the dream of total anarchy was over.

The Great Rock 'n' Roll Swindle, by director Julien Temple, was released in 1980 as a sort of fictional biopic about the Sex Pistols' rise to fame. Like a final epitaph to an impossible dream, the film covers the entire Cash from Chaos period and the eventual split of the band through the eyes of McLaren, the band's manager.

In the next decade, two more excellent films about the Punk period came out, and the Contemporary Wardrobe Collection supplied both these films with authentic Punk clothes, many of which feature in this chapter. The biopic Sid & Nancy: Love Kills, 1986, directed by Alex Cox, is about the life of Sex Pistols' bassist Sid Vicious and his girlfriend Nancy Spungen. And set in 1977, Young Soul Rebels, 1991, directed by Isaac Julien, captures the spirit of the emerging soul and Punk scenes.

Above: Green leather army coat, 1950s, Germany. Black button-down shirt, 1970s, London. Red and black tie, 1950s, USA.

Left: Fig 1. Grey cotton pilot's flying suit, 1960s, England. White cotton vest, Bundeswehr, 1970s, Germany. Black leather army boots, 1960s, England.

Fig 2. Green leather army coat, 1950s, Germany. Black button-down shirt, 1970s, London. Red and black tie, 1950s, USA. Black leather belt, 1970s, London. Black leather jodhpurs, 1950s, Germany. Black rubber riding boots, 1970s, London.

Vive Le Punk

In 1993 I re-housed the Contemporary Wardrobe Collection in an old Victorian Horse Hospital in Bloomsbury. I thought, what better way to launch the space than to hold a retrospective exhibition of Westwood & McLaren revolutionary Punk designs? I had amassed quite a collection of their clothes myself, but needed many more to tell the whole story. I systematically got in touch with lots of other collectors and old Punks I knew that had been around the scene at the time, who were also very knowledgeable, and they all agreed to contribute items. In the end we managed to gather together almost all representative items from their 1971–1978 collections.

Entitled *Vive Le Punk*, I wanted to present the exhibition theatrically in the true spirit of the McLaren Westwood shops. So we constructed about 30 pink vinyl body bags and hung them on red rope from the ceiling like meat carcasses, each dressed in thematic outfits. They were hanging at head height so you could actually touch the garments. Of course it was huge gamble, as well over 300 of London's glitterati and hardcore fans turned up for the private view, but everyone was incredibly respectful of the whole thing, and they absolutely loved the way it was displayed.

Everyone apart from a group of V&A curators, who were really shocked that the clothes were hung in such an unconventional manner, and horrified that people could actually touch them! But I had always felt that museums had outdated attitudes with their staid presentations, and this exhibition, in the true spirit of Punk, was the perfect opportunity to break the rules of traditional displays. Ironically the V&A were to emulate many elements of my displays the following year with their *Street Style* exhibition.

Although they had both endorsed the exhibition neither Malcolm nor Vivienne really wanted to come and see it. Malcolm was living in Paris furthering his musical career, while Vivienne stated that she was no longer solely interested in youth and street culture and was more inspired by tradition and technique. But I insisted that the exhibition was an important part of their heritage and perhaps the only time all their designs would ever be shown together in their entirety.

It took a great deal of persuasion and coercion to get them there, some ten years after they had split up, but at the last minute they both agreed to come the night before the private view, although they were quite shocked to see each other after such a long time. Needless to say the atmosphere that evening was electrifying, which thankfully I caught in its entirety on film. Both Vivienne and Malcolm were on fine form, reminiscing, debating and arguing about how, where and when they designed the collections. It was like witnessing a sparring match of memories and words playing out before my eyes, with Malcolm the most outspoken, reliving the past with his elaborate stories, and Vivienne carefully recounting her experiences in great detail, while putting Malcolm's wild tales into context.

Vive Le Punk proved to be a huge success with a great deal of TV and magazine coverage. The show attracted well over 3,000 visitors, from all over the world, and I was soon invited to create a similar but more general exhibition in Tokyo at the influential Shiseido Gallery the following year. The exhibition was called *Punkature* – after Vivienne's spring/summer 1983 collection, 'a futuristic interpretation of punk'. The show was featured in every fashion magazine and journal in Japan and went on to break all records for the space, attracting some 15,000 eager fans.

Arguably, Punk was the last great rebellious sub-culture to have been created and its spirit and legacy, especially in fashion circles, continues to this day. There also seems to be no end to the interest McLaren and Westwood's clothes from that period still generate, and I for one feel extremely privileged to have taken part in their remarkable journey.

Left: Fig 1. Pink Destroy print muslin top, Seditionaries, mid 1970s, London. Red tartan mini-kilt, mid 1970s, London. Black fishnet tights. Black strap bondage boots, Seditionaries, mid 1970s, London.

Fig 2. Red wool school blazer, mid 1970s, England. White cotton Sid Vicious I'm Yours print T-shirt, Seditionaries, late 1970s, London. White cotton bondage trousers, Seditionaries, mid 1970s, London. Black leather cut out boots, mid 1960s, England.

Left: Fig 1. White muslin top with Punk Hell print, Boy, late 1970s, London. Metal and leather belt and chain choker, mid 1970s, London. Red cotton stencilled trousers, mid 1970s, London. Black leather strap pointed toe boots, Ad Hoc, mid 1970s, London.

Fig 2. Cream calico bondage suit, mid 1970s, London. Red felt mini-kilt, Seditionaries, mid 1970s, London. Black and tan bondage boots, Seditionaries, late 1970s, London.

Previous page and right: Fig 1. Black cotton bondage coat, Seditionaries, mid 1970s, London. Striped cotton shirt, Seditionaries, mid 1970s, London. Black watch tartan wool trousers, mid 1960s, England. Black suede pointed toe boots, mid 1960s, England.

Fig 2. Black cotton parachute shirt, Seditionaries, mid 1970s, London. Black cotton bondage trousers, Seditionaries, mid 1970s, London. Black leather strap boots, Seditionaries, mid 1970s, London.

Fig 3. Black cotton bondage jacket, Seditionaries, mid 1970s, London. Black, green and ginger check wool trousers, 1970s, London. Black leather eight-eyelet boots, Dr. Martens, London.

Left: Fig 1. Black leather cross zip biker jacket, Blatt, 1950s, Chicago. Black studded Venus T-shirt remade by Joe Corré, Let it Rock, 1990s, London. White leather studded choker, studded metal chain belts, mid 1970s, London. Grey and black leopard print cotton mini-skirt, mid 1970s, London. Black fishnet tights. Black patent pointed toe lace-up witch's boots, mid 1970s, London.

Fig 2. Black leather biker jacket, 1970s, London. White cotton Expose print T-shirt, Seditionaries, late 1970s, London. Padlock and chain. Blue denim jeans, Levi's. Black and white canvas baseball boots, 1970s, London.

Right: Sid Vicious, *The Great Rock 'n' Roll Swindle*, dir Julien Temple, 1980.

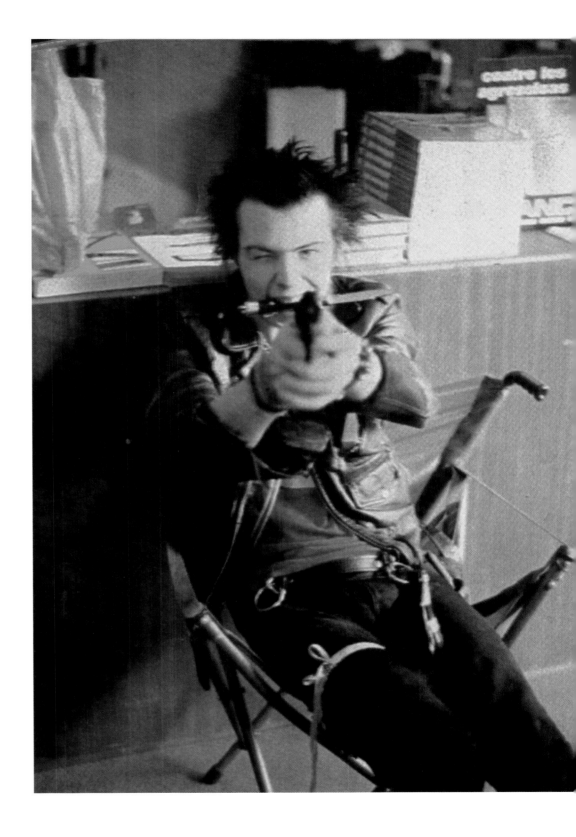

INDEX

*Page numbers in **bold***
refer to picture captions.

PICTURE CREDITS

The publishers wish to thank all the individuals and institutions who have provided photographic images for use in this book. In all cases, every effort has been made to contact copyright holders, but should there be any omissions the publishers would be pleased to insert the appropriate acknowledgement in any subsequent edition of the book.

Numbers refer to pages.

4 Courtesy Hugh Finnegan
12 Productions/REX/Shutterstock
14-15 Courtesy Warner Bros Pictures
18 PA Images
22 Getty Images/Bettmann
28 Getty Images/Archive Photos
34 Getty Images/John Springer Collection, Universal International Pictures
40 Mary Evans Picture Library, Headliner Productions
43 Getty Images / Life Images Collection
46 Courtesy of Charter Film Productions
52 Universal International Pictures
60-61 Getty Images/Picture Post, Romulus Film
62 Pictorial Press Ltd / Alamy Stock Photo, Romulus Film
68 Getty Images/George Konig
71 M. Everard
72-73 Mary Evans Picture Library, The Rank Organisation
76 Getty Images/Allan Grant, Wyatt Earp Enterprises
79 Courtesy Hugh Finnegan
80-81 Courtesy Hugh Finnegan
84 TopFoto/Ken Russell, Picture Post magazine
87 Mary Evans Picture Library
95 Museum of London
98-99 Columbia Pictures/Stanley Kramer Productions
102 Polaris Images/Life Magazine
109 © Karlheinz Weinberger, courtesy KHW-Foundation, 2017
115 Getty Images/Michael Ochs Archive, A Raymond Stross Production
127 Getty Images/Hulton Archive, American International Pictures (AIP)
128-129 Getty Images/Bill Ray
132 Universal/REX/Shutterstock, Universal International Pictures (UI)
134 Mary Evans Picture Library, Metro-Goldwyn-Mayer (MGM)
138 Photographer unknown, 'Paris by Night' Charles Skilton, 1959
149 Getty Images/Central Press
154 ©Leni Sinclair
158 Tricastle/Allied Artists International
162 Mary Evans Picture Library, Atlas Productions
165 Mary Evans Picture Library, Atlas Productions
171 ©Don McCullin/Contact Press Images
178 Courtesy Frank & Christine Nolan
180-181 Getty Images/Terence Spencer
190 George Konig/REX/Shutterstock
196 REX/Shutterstock, Mark Wingett, The Who Films
198-199 A Memorial Enterprises Film
200 Getty Images/Beverly Lebarrow
207 Camera Press
208 Colin Jones/Topham TopFoto.co.uk
213 Metro-Goldwyn-Mayer (MGM), A Joseph Janni Vic Films Production
225 Bill Orchard/REX/Shutterstock
230-231 Getty Images/Peter Stackpole
234 ©Lisa law
246 Mary Evans Picture Library, Michael Laughlin Enterprises, Universal Pictures
249 ©Leni Sinclair
250 Avalon Red, Columbia
252-253 Getty Images/Bettmann
258 Getty Images/Tony Russell
260 ITV/REX/Shutterstock, Central Independent Television
266 Getty Images/Keystone-France
268 Museum of London
271 Mirrorpix
276 Photographer Unknown
282 ©Gered Mankowitz
288-289 Whaley-Malin Productions, Megalovision
299 Ray Stevenson/REX/Shutterstock
302 Getty Images/Estate of Keith Morris
304 Getty Images/Erica Echenberg
321 Moviestore/REX/Shuttestock, Boyd's Co, Kendon Films, Matrixbest, Virgin Films
328 Productions/REX/Shutterstock

FURTHER READING

Hepsters Dictionary, Cab **Calloway**, 1939
On The Road, Jack Kerouac, 1957
Absolute Beginners, Colin **MacInnes**, 1959
Naked Lunch, William S. **Burrough's**, 1959
One Flew Over the Cuckoo's Nest, Ken **Kesey**, 1962
The Autobiography of Malcolm X, **Malcolm X**, 1965
Quant by Quant, Mary **Quant**, 1965
The Kandy-Kolored Tangerine-Flake Streamline Baby, Tom **Wolfe**, 1966
The Electric Kool-Aid Acid Test, Tom **Wolfe**, 1968
Revolt Into Style, George **Melly**, 1970
Skinhead, Richard **Allen**, 1970
Mods, Richard **Barnes**, 1979
Skinhead, Nick **Knight**, 1982
The Bowery Boys, David **Hayes** & Brent **Walker**, 1984
Ball The Wall, Nik **Cohn**, 1989
The Intrepid Traveler, Ken **Babbs**, 1990
On the Bus, Paul **Perry**, 1990
Hell's Angels, Yves **Lavigne**, 1993
Beat Culture and the New America 1950-1965, Lisa **Phillips**, 1996
Punk A Life Apart, **Colegrave & Sullivan**, 2001
Karl Heinz Weinberger photos 1954-1995, Andreas Zust **Verlag**, 2002
An Underworld at War, Donald **Thomas**, 2003
Mods The New Religion, Paul 'Smiler' **Anderson**, 2013

ESSENTIAL VIEWING

Angels with Dirty Faces, dir Michael Curtiz, 1938
Love Finds Andy Hardy, dir George B. Seitz, 1938
Gone With The Wind, dir Victor Fleming, 1939
Jitterbugs, dir Malcolm St Clair, 1943
Jammin' the Blues, dir Gjon Mili, 1944
Waterloo Road, dir Sidney Gilliat, 1945
Appointment with Crime, dir John Harlow, 1946
London Town, dir Wesley Ruggles, 1946
Brighton Rock, dir John Boulting, 1947
It Always Rains on Sunday, dir Robert Hamer, 1947
Good-Time Girl, dir David MacDonald, 1948
City Across the River, dir Maxwell Shane, 1949
The Blue Lamp, dir Basil Deardon, 1950
A Streetcar Named Desire, dir Elia Kazan, 1951
Cosh Boy, dir Lewis Gilbert, 1953
Roman Holiday, dir William Wyler, 1953
The Wild One, dir László Benedek, 1953
Girl Gang, dir Robert C. Dertano, 1954
Blackboard Jungle, dir Richard Brooks, 1955
Rebel Without a Cause, dir Nicholas Ray, 1955
Crime in The Streets, dir Donald Siegal, 1956
Rock Around the Clock, dir Fred F. Sears, 1956
The Girl Can't Help It, dir Frank Tashlin, 1956
The Violent Years, dir William Morgan, 1956
Funny Face, dir Stanley Donen, 1957
Jailhouse Rock, dir Richard Thorpe, 1957
Six-Five Special, TV Series, UK, 1957-1958
High School Confidential, dir Jack Arnold, 1958
Oh Boy!, TV Series, UK, 1958-1959
Pull my Daisy, dir Robert Frank, Alfred Leslie, 1959
The March to Aldermaston, dir Lindsey Anderson, 1959
Beat Girl, Edmond T. Greville, 1960
Breathless, Jean-Luc Godard, 1960
The Subterraneans, dir Ranald MacDougall, 1960
The Rebel, Robert Day, 1961
West Side Story, dir Jerome Robbins, Robert Wise, 1961
The Boys, dir Sidney J.Furie, 1962
Love with the Proper Stranger, dir Robert Mulligan, 1963
A Hard Day's Night, dir Richard Lester, 1964
Scorpio Rising, dir Kenneth Anger, 1964
The Leather Boys, dir Sidney J. Furie, 1964
The Cincinnati Kid, dir Norman Jewison, 1965
The Party's Over, dir Guy Hamilton, 1965
Wholly Communion, dir Peter Whitehead, 1965
Ready, Steady, Go!, TV Series, UK, 1963-1966
The Wild Angels, dir Roger Corman, 1966
Far From the Madding Crowd, John Schlesinger, 1967
Bonnie & Clyde, dir Arthur Penn, 1968
Bullitt, dir Peter Yates, 1968
If…, dir Lindsey Anderson, 1968
The Thomas Crown Affair, dir Norman Jewison, 1968
Easy Rider, dir Dennis Hopper, 1969
Stones In The Park, dir Leslie Woodhead, 1969
Performance, dir Donald Cammell, Nicolas Roeg, 1970
The Breaking of Bumbo, dir Andrew Sinclair, 1970
A Clockwork Orange, dir Stanley Kubrick, 1971
The Last Picture Show, dir Peter Bogdanovich, 1971
American Graffiti, dir George Lucas, 1973
Dressing for Pleasure, dir John Samson, 1977
Jubilee, dir Derek Jarman, 1978
The Great Rock 'n' Roll Swindle, dir Julien Temple, 1980
Made in Britain, TV, UK, dir Alan Clarke, 1983
Skinhead Farewell, TV, UK, 1996
The Filth and the Fury, dir Julien Temple, 2000

Many of the clothes illustrated in this book were featured in the following cult films:

Quadrophenia, dir Franc Roddam, 1978
The Ruttles: All You Need is Cash, dir Eric Idle, Gary Wies, 1978
The Birth of The Beatles, dir Richard Marquand, 1979
The Wall, dir Alan Parker, 1982
Dance With A Stranger, dir Mike Newell, 1985
Jazzin' For Blue Jean, dir Julien Temple, 1985
Absolute Beginners, dir Julien Temple, 1986
Little Shop of Horrors, dir Frank Oz, 1986
Sid & Nancy, dir Alex Cox, 1986
Comic Strip Presents: The Yob, dir Ian Eames, 1987
Great Balls of Fire, Jim McBride, 1989
The Commitments, dir Alan Parker, 1991
Young Soul Rebels, dir Isaac Julien, 1991
Vive Le Punk, dir Roger K. Burton, 1993
Hackers, Iain Softley, 1995
Stoned, dir Stephen Woolley, 2005
Worried About The Boy, dir Julian Jarrold, 2010

For more information visit **www.rebel-threads.com**

Acknowledgements

Some two years in the making, this book very much represents my life's work. The journey from concept to publication was at times a rapid learning curve, and in some ways harder than costuming a period movie, particularly as a photo is far more prone to close scrutiny. So I am extremely indebted to my brilliant team of creatives, who enthusiastically came on board from the outset and worked tirelessly throughout the process to turn a pipedream into reality.

I would especially like to thank James Lyndsey whose fabulous photography and stunning lighting captured the cinematic mood perfectly, and gave the clothes new life, and to my son Will, who translated my vision of the book beautifully, while taking it to another level with his wonderfully stylish yet timeless design, that is a fitting testament for all our hard work. Many thanks also to Laura Nash whose creative input, careful preparation and calmness throughout assured that the shoots were a smooth and hugely enjoyable process.

I would like to express my sincere thanks to everyone else who contributed to this book. In particular, Kate Forbes, Brian Griffin, Ken Hollings, Lloyd Johnson, Laurence King, Mark Pilkington, Tai Shani, Mike Crawford, Chris Symes, Julien Temple, Cathi Unsworth and Marketa Uhlirova, who all shared freely their time, knowledge, advice, support and expertise.

My gratitude also goes to Guy Adams, Reagan Clare, Sholto Dobie, Rod Hamlin, Alix Marie, Paul Spencer, Emma Barker, Stevie Bennett, Catherine Smith, Rachel Lawson, Emma Kate-Wood and Kyle Zeto for their valuable input. Many thanks also to Piers Garland, whose fine detail shots feature in Chapter 6.

This book is dedicated to my amazing wife Izabel, forever a true rebel and constant source of spiritual inspiration.

Roger K. Burton

Portrait by James Lyndsay.

Scorpio Rising, dir Kenneth Anger, 1964.